BEYOND FOREVER
Unlocking the Door to Eternal Life

The Unveiling of the
Pure Mind Spiritual Practice.
"The Definitive Path Enabling
Perpetual Existence."

Compiled and edited by the
Pure Mind Foundation

Wheelbarrow Publishing
1632 Virginia Drive
Manhattan, Kansas 66502
SAN 299-7126

Copyright © 1998 by Pure Mind Foundation

All rights reserved. No part of this book may be reproduced or utilized in any form or by any means, electronic or mechanical, including photocopying, recording, or by any information storage and retrieval system, without written permission from the publisher.

ISBN 0-9666854-0-7

Library of Congress Catalog Card Number 98-87504

First Edition   10 9 8 7 6 5 4 3 2 1

For subscription information, questions concerning this book or the Pure Mind Practice, please turn to the back of the book.

Pure Mind Foundation
http://www.puremind.net
puremind@networksplus.net

Jacket concept: S.A.Stitz
Artist: Bridgit Steir
Graphics and design: S & N Design

Table of Contents

Foreword
Preface

Part One: Turning Towards Home
Chapter One
   "No man truly knows himself"
Chapter Two
   Cleansing My Mind
Chapter Three
   In Silence

Part Two: Opening Your Spiritual Eye
Summary: In a Nutshell
Introduction
Ideology — Universal Truths
Chapter Four
   The Pure Mind Path
      an overview
Chapter Five
   The Universal Life Wheel
Chapter Six
   Awaking to the Pure Mind
   Ideal Through Meditation
Chapter Seven
   Our Living Practice
Chapter Eight
   The Heart and Soul
      of Pure Mind Practice
      love, kindness, compassion, and sensitivity

Chapter Nine
> *Mindfulness*

Chapter Ten
> *Pure Mind Understanding*
>> Reincarnation, Creation,
>> Life as an In-Perpetuum Being,
>> The Breath of Universal Life,
>> Suffering, Awakening Energy,
>> The Final Life Moment

Chapter Eleven
> *Right Living*

Chapter Twelve
> *Awakening the Unknown*

Chapter Thirteen
>> Energy in Relation to
>> Motion and Space

Part Three: The Answers Most Readily Sought, and Other Topics of Interest

Most modern day religions have an approximate date of "birth." How old is the practice of which you speak?

Are there other books or scholars I can consult on the subject of becoming In-Perpetuum?

If teachers or mentors are so crucial, why are they not readily available to most seekers?

What is the Universal Cycle?
Can you explain the similarity of near-death experiences?

How should humans judge the meaning of their lives?

Isn't my nature different from yours? If not, how do you understand the word nature?

Other than the obvious long-term benefits of this practice, are there any advantages in the present life?

Turning inward, does one have to take a vow of poverty?

Are teachers and prophets of other disciplines likely to be reincarnated?

Meeting an In-Perpetuum teacher, what should one's aim be?

If, after studying with a teacher for a while, he were to pass on, who will guide my practice?

I have become totally confused with the use of the word enlightenment; can you clarify its meaning?

Most of the hierarchy in the popular world religions are very exposed. Why do In-Perpetuum Beings conceal themselves?

You have said many times that logical thought is a barrier to contact with spiritual dimensions and understandings; can you give me an example of this?

Can you express to me in words your experiences and feelings about the Pure Mind Path's Life Practice?

You speak of different energy groups. Do any of these fall into what people refer to as the spirit world?

I have heard the expression "clear seeing" as a way to understand "suchness or itness." Could you explain it further?

Are all the rituals necessary for a spiritual practice to be meaningful?

I gather there is nothing we should take to our pillows. Is that correct?

Without a teacher or guide and with no community nearby, how does one start to practice?

Have you had a student who has failed, and if so, what were the reasons?

Many times I find that I need a glossary of terms and words to understand what Zen commentators are trying to say. Why don't they speak to us in words we can easily understand?

There seem to be many paths or disciplines that expect a herd mentality from their students. They therefore teach a strict set of rules and rituals to be followed in order to reach enlightenment. Does the Pure Mind Path differ?

Emptiness is a concept I find hard to understand. Could you comment on its value?

In what form will an In-Perpetuum Being reveal himself to me?

How do you answer the people who insist that each person must find his own way?

What do you feel is the greatest difference in the approach of a Pure Mind student and those of other practices or religions?

All that you have said is very exciting and different, but how can I know that it's true?

Part Four: Additional Topics and Miscellaneous Ranting
    A Letter to a Friend
    God
    The Christ
    Glossary

Afterword

ACKNOWLEDGMENT

A stream in order to cross over the deep engulfing waters of the stagnant lake must give himself up (surrender) to the sun so that the wind can carry him across and deposit him on the lush fruit bearing mountain top across the way. From there the reborn stream will flow with eternity.

To our teacher (the sun), the Truth of our practice (the wind), our families, fellow students, friends, our deeply felt gratitude for their patience and tolerance. Thank you.

Pure Mind Editors (the stream)

Warning-Disclaimer

This book was compiled to provide information about Pure Mind spiritual practice. It is sold with the understanding that the author, publisher, and editors are not engaged in rendering religious, sectarian, or psychological professional services. If any one or related services are required, seek the help of competent professionals.

It is not the purpose of this book to print all the information that is available to the author, publisher, or editors, but to provide a beginning text of spiritual understanding and path as practiced by Mahan Agass. You are urged to read all the available material to learn as much as possible about that which you feel suits your individual need concerning spirituality and the meaning for life. For more information, check your local library and bookstores.

The Pure Mind Path or any true spiritual practice is not a quick fix method. Anyone who decides to enter into this practice must expect to invest a lifetime of study and effort. For many of us the Pure Mind Path is much more rewarding than any known religious undertaking, and we have experienced tremendous growth and a continuously fulfilling way of life.

Every effort has been made to make this work as complete in its intent and as accurate as possible. However there may be mistakes both typographical and in content. Therefore this work should be used as a general guide and not as the ultimate source, because that can only come from within you. Furthermore, this text contains information on the beginning practice only up to the printing date.

The purpose of this book is to educate and inspire. The author, publisher, and editors shall have neither liability nor responsibility to any person or entity with respect to any loss or damage, of any nature, caused, or alleged to be caused, directly or indirectly by the information contained in this book or received by any other means of communication.

If you do not wish to be bound by the above, you may return this book, in a normal used condition, to the publisher for a full refund.

FOREWORD

Based on the unique experiences of an American traveling and working in Nepal who was by chance identified as a reincarnated ancient Tibetan monk of high spiritual attainment, this remarkable work describes his efforts to confirm his new identity as Mahan Agass, explore its significance, and ultimately, to accept responsibility for it by revealing many of the visionary insights that eventually awakened in him.

Most of the text has apparently been compiled by a small group within the Pure Mind Foundation, and some of it will appear arbitrary or even offensive to readers unfamiliar with the tantric traditions of Tibetan Buddhism and Hinduism. But much of the material speaks directly to the concerns of all metaphysical "seekers" or practitioners of spiritual disciplines. Particularly noteworthy are critical discussions of the limitations of organized Western religions, and especially of Japanese and North American Zen practices.

Although the criticisms of Zen are in many respects similar to those available in the writings of Krishnamurti, and more recently in Steven Batchelor's *Buddhism Without Beliefs,* they have obviously been developed independently and are offered more in a spirit of amplification than denigration. Indeed, Mahan Agass himself acknowledges some benefit from zazen meditation, but only to the extent that it opened the way to a metaphysical path leading beyond Zen.

By defying the accepted conventional wisdom of the human life cycle, Mahan Agass presents the most challenging theme of this book: identification of the universal form of spiritual existentialism transcending the boundaries of all religions. No mere cultist proclamation, it is presented with detailed instructions for its attainment, and in a rhetoric of authentic passion. Thus, the testimony of an "eternal energy vessel" mechanism that can be acquired by the means outlined in the text may appear excessively esoteric, but it gains plausibility when viewed in the context of quantum theory and Jung's theory on the collective unconscious. In sum, many readers will probably find this book's challenge to Western rationality uniquely unsettling, though not impossible to accept. I suspect, that like me, very few will find it easy to forget.

Leon Rappoport, PhD
Professor of Psychology
Co-author of *The Holocaust* and *The Crisis of Human Behavior,* author of *Human Judgment and Social Interaction, Personality Development: The Chronology of Experience,* and *Zen Running,* to name a few. Practitioner and student of zazen meditation for over twenty years.

Preface

It is because the human mind and heart crave that something which is much greater and more beautiful than its present state of mental and physical suffering, limited metaphysical understanding, and myriad of unanswered questions, that striving for and attaining the spiritual dimensions is revered and sought by prophets, seers, and religious scholars alike. This continuous craving which underlies man's motivation and endeavors we call "the hungry ghost."

The Pure Mind Path of awakening driven by Universal Nature and by its virtue of right practice throughout one's life is the veritable path beyond this human condition to awakening, receiving, and maintaining an eternal state ***In-Perpetuum.***

> ~The Way beyond,
> A lone traveler,
> they are I.~

Before you start on your journey through this record of modern day reawakening and awakenings, we'd like to express our frustration in attempting to find a word that combines the male and female genders without using a plural form such as "they." So where we speak of he, him, she, or her, it is meant to be nongeneric, merely a person.

Mention of any group, religion, or person does not imply our endorsement of their activities or spirituality.

The phenomenal potential that Pure Mind practice provides clearly suggests that it is worthwhile for you to lay aside all preconceptions before your evaluation. See it as emptying your cup of all coffee before it can be filled with pure white cream. Leaving even a drop of black coffee taints the cream and you can never fully taste, see, nor appreciate the cream's purity.

There are secrets spoken of and sometimes not explained in these pages. We do not intend this as an affront, but simply as protection for all of us. For example, when we speak of advanced meditation techniques, the why of their secrecy should be clear as you learn of their power.

On the other hand, another age-old secret is revealed, we believe, for the first time ever. We divulge an In-Perpetuum Being's ability to transfer a pure energy vessel to a lay person. This act bestows the lay person or student/disciple with the necessary vehicle to become an eternal being without actually having personally achieved it. It should be very clear to everyone why reincarnates have never revealed this ability to the general populace before. We write of this because we know from firsthand experience that it is true, and it is also a part of Mahan's awakening to do so. At this point in man's evolution, it was hard for him to understand the necessity of divulging this information, but through further reawakening enlightenments he understood. He also makes it clear why it is very necessary to practice before and after receiving the eternal life-sustaining vessel.

Awakenings cannot be counted on to arise upon necessity, or more to the point, at a time convenient to the continuity of this record. It may, therefore, seem to the reader that we have neglected to maintain an even flow for his ease of understanding, and that we have repeated ourselves somewhat throughout. But for us to alter the awakenings as they came or change the verbiage for the sake of an easily readable structure seems beside the point and not necessarily the correct choice.

For the most part, we believe, you will be able to separate his reawakening and awakening experiences from his commentaries by his style, attitude, and use of words. But to make it very clear, we begin and end his awakenings with these ~:marks~:~.

You will be able to recognize in this record many of the "golden threads" that run through most of the world's respected religions. With Pure Mind awakening you will find many overwhelming differences, the primary ones being: why we are or the true purpose of our existence, and how we go about fulfilling that purpose.

The name Mahan Agass was first bestowed upon him by an oracle from Tibet, a person you will read about in chapter one.

We have taken the liberty of interspersing his prose, free verse, and poetry throughout this book. We did this because they are, for the most part, directly related to his awakenings and life experiences as they pertain to this book. They appear between these ~marks~.

Reincarnation, transmigration of souls, metempsychosis, rebirth, etc. differ, for the most part, in definition from our usage of the word reincarnate (-ation, -ed). These concepts, believed to have originated in the Indian subcontinent by Buddhists and others, is that our souls have lived before in other physical forms as human or non-human animals, and after death will, in due course, automatically be reincarnated into yet another form. This should be seen as diametrically opposed to Universal Nature's design of perpetual life that is addressed in this work. The defining difference being: perpetual life forms exist because humans warranted, therefore, attracted and polarized an eternal energy vessel that will not dissipate upon their physical death. This is in direct opposition to the concept of automatic rebirth. Others, like Plato, whose "middle period" dialogues present "philosophical proofs" of pre-existence of the human soul but offer no claims to pre-existence in any other material form, help prove that knowledge of eternal life runs far and deep throughout history. Today, any knowledge of eternal life is greatly misunderstood, and in many cases taken advantage of in the name of religion.

~in perfect clarity
I see the unclear,
clearly.~

It is not our inclination or desire to prove or defend in a scholarly manner the awakenings described in this book as some might expect. Research into some other persons' commentaries, awakenings, propositions, arguments, opinions or beliefs are all beside the point. To quote Mahan, "A person who adds another's words to prove his own credibility lacks conviction, a deep inner faith, and his spiritual enlightenment should be seen as questionable." It is impossible to defend newly awakened enlightenment experiences with old precepts. But, with careful examination and by using as a basic premise the presence of In-Perpetuum Beings, one will finally be able to root out all of the "golden threads" presently left dangling by modern day religions and spiritual practices.

It has been pointed out to him (and us) time and again that there could be, and therefore will be, many misconceptions about his use of the words "create, creator, energizer," etc., in all their various forms and ways. He would tell you up front that In-Perpetuum Beings are *nothing special*. When a human creates a beautiful piece of music or a painting or writes a great novel, he creates out of his nature, his human nature to do so. We may place a "special" label on him, but in fact he is just fulfilling his own natural desire with his ability. Human nature impregnated with his heredity provided his longing, his desire, and his ability to do so. When an In-Perpetuum Being energizes a latent possibility, he creates because he is fulfilling Universal Nature's desire to know itself. So, as with the human "creator," he is nothing special; he is just what his nature and his state of spiritual attainment dictate him to be. Being special is just in the mind of the observer, and one of our great practices as humans is not to be taken in by, nor act upon, such definitions that come from logical minds that house very limited awakened truths and understandings.

A word of advice. If you are looking for a practice that will set you apart and make you special by helping you rise above anything other than your own humanity, know now that you are looking in the wrong direction. If you believe ~:attaining eternal reincarnation is other than a normal state, you will not even begin to approach it.~:~

To comply with Mahan Agass' wishes and strong insistence, most of the extraordinary events, relationships, and experiences of his life have been omitted from the biographical sketch contained in the first three chapters. The time frame in those chapters has also been consolidated. This was agreed upon in the interest of ensuring privacy for both Mahan Agass and the persons who helped create or shared those remarkable and rare experiences.

We are made aware of our need for "assimilation" with something residing far beyond ourselves by our insatiable longing we call our "hungry ghost."

mahan agass

Part One

Turning Towards Home

*~Shadows lengthening
you won't appear
only echoes~*

There was something before any Gods, before the universes, before all form, and before all life. Quiet and still, pure and deep, timeless and spaceless it stands on its own and will not change. It cannot be bound by definition, it is the essence and energy of Universal Nature...................

Chapter One

"No man truly knows himself."
unknown

*"If for just one moment we could
see the face of our longing
we'd be set free."*

The following three chapters are transcripted from various talks introducing Mahan Agass to those who did not know of him or his background. One was delivered at a two week spiritual retreat in the Far East. The theme: *"The Spiritual Mind; Is it Possible?"* About one hundred fifty persons of high spiritual awareness were in attendance. The balance were delivered in the U.S.A.

"When the seeker is prepared the answers will come."

chapter one — Turning Towards Home

I never intended for my life, my reawakening, or my new awakenings to be made public. I simply kept a record of the incredible events that led me to my true identity and reawakening. I see my awakenings as a means for my work, not as an end of my work. The object of this record is evidence of my awakening, not something worthy of praise or admiration.

Being told by others that I was a reincarnate of a high spiritual being turned my life into a quest of proving or disproving their belief. This concept was foreign in nature and beyond anything known to me. Even though it might have seemed absurd, I had this strong haunting feeling: what if it were true? And if so, what did it truly mean? After my decision to pursue the truth, my first step was a search for a methodology, books, religion, and/or a teacher who could help me find the answers. Now when I think back on my life and specifically that time, I believe seeking to know and define myself was, in great part, the reason for my restless behavior which directed me down many a blind and foolish alley. "No man truly knows himself" proved an understatement in my case!

I have now come to know that I was, by choice, reincarnated to a middle class family in New York City, U.S.A. In their youth, most reincarnates are not aware of their place in Universal Nature's framework, but as they age they become appreciative of the difference in their perceptive abilities in comparison to others. These differences invariably remain unexplained, but usually are intensely studied, and until a reasonable explanation can be found, the reincarnate's family finds varied excuses for their child's odd behavior and thinking. My childhood was as thus, and as with the majority of teenagers in the nineteen fifties, New York life was very exciting. With the rebellion against all that was the establishment, led by the advent of rock and roll, the beat movement which evolved into "flower children" and further to "hippies," life proved to be a steady flow of music and close physical and mental relationships. As I was later to learn, my reincarnation definition was to be reborn into this stimulating generation, enjoying the best of this earth's incredible era. Life was especially dynamic and rewarding for me because of my heightened senses and perception into the human psyche. This resulted in many very satisfying and fulfilling relationships. Even though not understood by me at the time, my abilities with energy creation, placement, and movement along with a piercing insight into people's thinking and feelings created quite a stir.

With the exception of the very popular rock and roll singing group I sang with, I was basically a solitary person. After graduation from high school

chapter one — Turning Towards Home

I had no interest in pursuing scholastic or subjective knowledge "about" or "of" things; my interests lay purely "in" things which I knew instinctively to be permanently transformative. I served in the U.S. Army, married, and had a daughter by the age of thirty. My life until my mid-thirties was fairly normal, but it was strongly emphasizing a myriad of unanswered questions. I seemed to believe beyond a shadow of a doubt that all knowledge beyond what was known was indeed available, and had the sense that it was mine for the asking. I knew that the day was coming when I would have to pursue the deeper meaning of my and all other life forms. A wake up call from nature to go into the wilderness and pursue the reality of the interdependency of all being told me it was time.

A few years' backpacking deep into the mountains and forests as well as diving into the depths of the seas and oceans was preparation to meet the challenge pulling me to explore the mysterious East. I chose Nepal as my first destination. My immediate search was for freedom—freedom from the ever present feeling that life had meaning beyond the human condition. At that time I had no awareness of awakening or reawakening, but the pull to turn inward for answers away from a self-indulgent materialistic life was becoming very strong.

This is the way for reincarnates, though not all have the same time frame of reawakening. Some reawaken within the first year of their new form, and some very late in the normal life span of whatever form they're in. Ultimately, there are three reasons why Perpetual Beings are reincarnated. The first is to experience and judge the evolution progression of the present time in which they have returned, so adjustments, if needed, will be made by their definition and energy. The second is to define or recognize new possibilities so they may be energized into creation after the In-Perpetuum Being passes. The third is to define their next reincarnation. As will be shown later, this is possible only in their second reincarnation and all those thereafter.

During my first visit to Nepal I came under suspicion as a reincarnate by a group of Tibetan refugees when I was drawn to a certain object in a Tibetan antique shop. When I asked to see more items, the shopkeeper asked me to the back store room where I proceeded to select, out of many thousands, only items that were of enormous spiritual and religious significance. These pieces had been smuggled out of Tibet when China invaded. They came from the cave of a hermit monk who was considered to be possibly the highest spiritual being on earth in the period 650 to 708 C.E. The fact that I chose only pieces from this cave made the Tibetans suspicious, but their suspicions were not made known to me at that time.

When I returned from my scheduled trek into the Annapurna region twenty-six days later, I had a visitor at my hotel. Recognizing him as being from the antique shop, I accepted his invitation to meet some people of "high rank." It was at this secret meeting that I learned who they believed I was.

Seated in an outdoor pavilion at three o'clock in the morning were two Buddhist priests from Tibet. They were wearing their traditional red and yellow hats. Also present were three Hindu mystics from India, a Yogi guru with two disciples, a Tibetan hermit monk oracle, a Buddhist priest from Thailand accompanied by four monks, and eight to twelve Buddhist priests and monks from Nepal, as well as the original people from the antique store. After introductions were made by a monk who spoke English, I was told that most of the people there had traveled a great distance in secret to meet and speak with me, and if I didn't mind they would explain "all" after the few questions they had were satisfactorily answered by me. The anxiety that I felt was set aside with the hope of some straightforward answers that were being promised. Actually only a few questions were posed. The first one asked was my birth time and date. When I answered, the oracle went directly to a very large and old looking book and seemed to fall into deep concentration as he studied certain pages.

The next question had to do with "any seemingly mysterious, mystical, or unexplained events that took place in my life." This was followed with, "Why did you choose the items you did at the Tibetan store?" I answered the question about "mysterious events" by relating and demonstrating two specific examples of my ability to create a forceful energy field and move or place it where I chose. I next told of a recent experience in the Himalayas when I awoke one morning to see the clouds drifting endlessly in the sky and saw clearly that the surrounding mountains were also flowing endlessly. Overwhelmed by this awakening experience, I had cried uncontrollably, because at that moment I understood that all life forms, everything, was impermanent. Amongst other events I revealed was one that took place at a facility where I was being fingerprinted by the F.B.I. for a license. It was mentioned by two different people, one of whom was a fingerprint expert, the other a historian, that I had very unusual print patterns (actually they were more specific but I will not reveal that information) that had been seen only a few times since the advent of fingerprinting as a means of identification. It was also explained that the other sets were from world renowned spiritual leaders. As for the articles I chose at the store, my only explanation was that they were things I was attracted to and felt I should have. I was then asked to choose which disk necklace, from three, was the one I chose at the store. After handling all three I stated, "None are the one I had in my hands before." Without a hint from anyone as to whether I was correct, they placed the items back into a carved wooden box.

At this point the oracle came to my side with the book he had been studying and proceeded to tell me that by the sacred calendar I was born in the dragon year, in the dragon month, on the dragon day, and at the dragon hour. Then he asked if I knew the significance of the dragon, and I replied, "He has a bad reputation in the Christian religion as a sign of the devil and in mythology as an ogre." A lot of laughter followed. Then the priest in the red hat told me that in the Buddhist religion and in Sanskrit, dragon translates into "awakened one,î the very same definition as the word Buddha, and is therefore used as a synonym for the historical Buddha as well as all those having reached the deepest or highest state of enlightenment. The oracle spoke up again and told me something pertaining to my numerology charts which he claimed revealed much about my past and future. The red hat priest then proceeded to tell me that they all believed that I was the reincarnate of this hermit monk of whom they spoke. When I asked if that could be proven, the priest replied that all the physical and what little mental evidence I had given showed this to be true, but the only true way for me to know would be through my own awakening experience of that fact, and for that matter, any other reincarnations I might have had since or before.

There was a bit more that took place that morning, but those were the most significant details. It was dawn in an instant, or so it seemed, and most of the group expressed, though regretfully, the need to get some sleep before leaving for their secret journeys home on that very day. There was much bowing of different styles and wishes for the future. Most of the "higher ranking" persons offered some advice and/or thoughts to me in private as they were departing. Some of what was offered was: "learn to focus your mind," "study the Buddha precepts," "you must pursue your reawakening in order to awaken your purpose," and by the oracle, "you will embody in this lifetime who you are," "follow your heart," from a Nepalese priest, "please return as soon as possible," and from the red hat priest, "please try to make a prolonged stop in Thailand on your way home to visit the temples in Bangkok, and plan a side trip to India on your anticipated return to Asia." With that said he placed a small traditional Tibetan bag in my hands, bowed deeply, and departed.

Back at the hotel I spent the rest of the early morning in a daze-like state thinking about the night's events. It wasn't until I thought of going to lunch at Mike's Breakfast that I remembered the bag. Opening it I found the disk necklace I had first discovered in the shop along with a note that said, "This astrological necklace we know was worn by you about thirteen hundred years ago, and it is our honor to return it to its owner."

I was able to schedule a stopover in Bangkok, but not for a prolonged time. It was a very hot and windless day, a spell that had been heavily felt for the past four days. None of the temples' bells which hung from the roofs on the palace grounds had rung during this period; it was that still. Entering the Temple of the Jade Buddha I was greeted by three Buddhist priests, one being the red hat priest from Tibet. The temple was filled with tourists and devotees so we four sat on the floor in silence for about one half-hour. The Tibetan priest then asked to be alone with me for a few minutes. We retired to a rear room where we spoke briefly about my plans to visit again, where and when, for me to be sure to leave time for a trip to India, and that monks would make the arrangements from Kathmandu. I agreed to return in six months. The two of us stepped outside where there were about two thousand monks all seated up against the temples' walls. They all bowed, and the bells on all the temples' roofs rang and continued to ring well beyond the time I left the grounds. Still there was no sign of any breeze.

I returned to Kathmandu, six months to the day later. Except for my numerous visits to Buddhist and Hindu temples in and around Kathmandu the only noteworthy events were the arm's length attention I was getting from the monks and priests of various temples who either sensed or knew of me, and of course, the two magnificent treks I joined into the Himalayas high country.

Between treks, arrangements had been made for me to go to India, and I was accompanied by an Indian Buddhist monk. While in India I met with, by invitation, the person I, at that time, believed to be the highest spiritual person in physical form today. We walked through gardens and spoke of many seemingly insignificant things, but the one thing he said that was directed to my new found life was, "Compassion is the foundation of all that's truth; this is where you should start your journey." The meeting lasted about forty minutes. I was then shown the rest of the grounds and was formally introduced to two young tulkus (Buddhist definition: reincarnates having attained a high spiritual state in a former life) of Indian birth and many of the hierarchy of the Buddhist religion. I was later invited to meet and speak with the same aforementioned high spiritual person a couple of years later in America, which I did.

Now convinced that my life was indeed meant for something other than indulging in worldly pleasures, I began my search. For three years, more or less, I spoke about and read everything I could regarding religious philosophy and philosophy in general. I spoke only to those who appeared to have an open mind, and these proved to be very, very few, indeed. But mainly I was preparing my mind to turn inward, becoming thoroughly convinced there could not be any other way. Hinduism, Sufism, Buddhism, Islam, Zen, and a few other traditions gave me the concepts of insight meditation and so I began to sit in silence. Being a reincarnate I quickly overcame the usual physical problems and mental activity that normally accompany all beginners in their first few years of meditation practice. In most cases the quieting of their minds is never "really" achieved. I accomplished both in less than three months. Also of interest was the amazement, of some, of how easily I grasped and understood the complex, perplexing, and intricate writings, poetry, sutras, and commentaries of certain religions' disciplines and practices. But to me all Truth was becoming clear, my veils were again being lifted, and this was only the beginning.

All this did not happen overnight, nor with the apparent ease I may have led you to believe.

Therefore, I feel that a look at the beginning of my practice might bring comfort to those who will struggle, while for those lucky ones who progress easily, it should provide a good belly laugh.

~Sitting quietly at twilight I was surrounded by the forces of melodic chanting. A monk in deep meditation enraptured my heart as he appeared to, just for a moment, transcend form and become pure white energy. Now and forever I remain intimately connected to him whenever lightning strikes at dusk.~

<small>Witnessed at the "monkey temple" in Kathmandu, Nepal</small>

Chapter Two

~Prayer flags beating
in the wind
cleanse our minds~

"Enlightenment is like the moon reflected on the water. The moon does not get wet, nor is the water broken. Although its light is wide and great, the moon is reflected even in a puddle an inch wide. The whole moon and the entire sky are reflected in one dew drop."

Dogen

chapter two — *Cleansing My Mind*

Living in a small Christian-based American midwestern city, I knew that I would be at a disadvantage in my search for a practice. Fortunately the town contained a state university of some size and a better than average public library. With those institutions and the Internet, I was able to garner a great deal of information through books and cyberspace. I devoured everything I could find in regard to the Eastern religions. What I found was that were are certain threads of philosophical understanding and acceptance that rang true within each. This did not make my choice for a practice any easier. I did and still do believe that life is never at a standstill, but what I wanted was to study and practice that which had not changed much since its inception or at least since the seventh century. I further believed that if I truly wanted to attract and awaken to whom I was reincarnated from, I would have to learn and understand the disciplines of the era I previously had lived.

My search was proving that spiritual practices and religions grow and develop into something far removed from their origin and intent. In today's society religions depend on mass appeal, a dynamic leader, and the gathering of funds, and that is where a great deal of their life force is directed. I needed a spiritual practice that repeated the cycles of those practitioners who came before. My criterion was that if the being I was reincarnated from were to drop in on me as I practiced, he should recognize what I was doing and not be totally confused as Jesus and Buddha would be if they were to drop in on churches bearing their respective names. Yes, individuals and groups change, but I felt that no true and successful search into the realms of spirituality could remain pure with indiscriminate change. Especially today, when change takes place for the sake of mass appeal, it is invariably the esoteric qualities that suffer. This is not to say that the people responsible were aware of the damage they were causing. Of course, I am judging and interpreting modern changes based on my awakening to Universal Truth.

True believers in the evolved Pure Land School of Buddhism (amongst others) are considered heretics throughout the other Buddhist communities; but correct understanding of Buddha and further enlightenment to Truth clearly show that they are all heretics to a large degree.

Returning to my problem at hand, having convinced myself of the necessity to find the perfect "practice" to complement the advice I had been given in Nepal ("to follow the Buddha way"), and being further convinced that my former life had been in Tibet, I arrived at the obvious conclusion to study Tibetan Buddhism and follow its practice methods. Armed with sutras, mantras, and ritual practice instruments, I began my practice. This proved to be a short-lived, painful, frustrating experience which had the effect of strengthening my rebelling ego! This is not meant to criticize what could be an excellent beginning practice, but with no one except faceless (therefore fearless), ego-driven, self-proclaimed Buddhist experts in cyberspace to discuss my practice with, I became disheartened. Even I recognized that spirituality cannot begin with the letter "I".

Skimming through a local Free University catalogue, I spotted a three-day lecture on Zen Buddhism meditation. Sadly, I was going to be out of town on the first two days, but I was hoping to attend on the third night. I called the professor/lecturer to make arrangements. Not having heard of a Zen Buddhist group in all the years I lived there, I asked him if there was a group sitting locally. "Yes," he said, "and you are welcome to join us, but you should be prepared to sit quietly for one or two forty-minute periods, and you should bring a pillow to sit on." With further inquiry I found that the group followed the Soto tradition of Zen. Since there was quite a bit written about this tradition, I was familiar with it. Retracing my steps, I began a review of Soto Zen starting with *moon in a dewdrop, writings of zen master dogen*, edited by Kazuaki Tanahashi. When I had first read this work, comprised mostly of Dogen's essays, it truly captured my imagination and whet my appetite for Zen.

There were two reasons why I had previously decided not to practice in this tradition. First, because it was developed in Japan in the 1200's and, therefore, not Tibetan in nature; and second, because everything else (fairly extensive) I had read written by its later practitioners and scholars seemed shallow and uninspiring. The exception was Shunryu Suzuki's Zen Mind, Beginner's Mind, which was simple, yet at times insightful. But again, as in most religions, the later day followers of Zen were often untrue to the original founding principles. Holding on to the inspirations I received from Dogen and in search of advice, I packed under my arms my colorful couch cushions and was off to a makeshift schoolroom "zendo."

> In autumn
> even though I may
> see it again,
> how can I sleep
> with the moon this evening? Dogen

As I am sure some of you will agree, going home can sometimes be a slow and painful experience. My journey started in earnest just like my first backpacking adventure; I brought the wrong equipment and never bothered to learn how to adjust myself to it. My technique was sloppy, and my mind was not at all prepared for the long haul. Arriving at the zendo I was not only concerned with my back and knee problems (which were medals from playing physical sports when I was younger and which seemed to be deteriorating further), but I also felt it necessary to keep what I had been told in Nepal a secret.

I was the first to arrive; it was 5:15 AM on a Monday, and so I sat in what looked like someone's old living room complete with fireplace. Soon a tall, imposing man walked in carrying a small duffel bag and a metal tool type box. Without a glance in my direction, he proceeded through a door and up a flight of stairs. Taking off his shoes, he bowed and entered a room filled with long tables and many chairs; I followed. He proceeded to lay out his black cushion and pillow; then he took a candle, incense burner, framed picture of a Buddhist priest, and a small statue of Buddha from the tool box and placed them on a windowsill, transforming it into an altar. He pointed to a spot on the floor which I took to be where I was to sit, so I laid down my pillows keeping one eye on him for any sign of disapproval. Remembering that the period would be in silence, I resolved just to follow as closely as I could every move that was being made.

We sat down in the Zen Soto way and did some stretching exercises, alone together. A few minutes later someone else came in. It was very dark with just a single flame from the candle on the sill, so I couldn't see who it might be. He and I stood up, and the three of us did ten full Japanese style bows, first to our knees, then to the floor. Finally seated, we waited until he lit a piece of incense and hit a small gong three times as a call to start the ancient practice of zazen, the Zen method of silent sitting meditation.

Looking back now, I outright laugh at myself for what must have appeared to others as it does to me now: my comedic attempt simply to sit. Since I felt I could not sit upright unless my back was supported, I started my sit with my legs in the half lotus position facing the room with my back up against the wall. Peeking at the others I saw that they were facing the wall as I had read they would. I say I "started out" sitting this way, because it was only five minutes before I moved my right leg to the quarter lotus, and another seven or so before I changed to the Burmese variation. My one solace as the others sat perfectly still was that I was able to change positions silently, I thought, without disturbing them. Before the gong sounded many hours later, or so it seemed, I was sitting with both of my legs stretched out, my hands behind my back up against the wall, and my mind racing to coffee. We then, gratefully, repeated three of the beginning bows to the altar, formed a circle, and further bowed to each other. After packing and bowing our way out of the room, they introduced themselves and expressed their delight in having me there. If I chose to come, the next sit would be Wednesday at 5:30 AM; they would be there for two forty-minute sits with a ten-minute walking meditation in between. Actually I think it was their warm and nonjudgmental attitude that helped me decide later that day to return.

But, for the time being, coffee was my only priority, so I rushed home and prepared double what I normally drank. My body ached and my mind was flashing pictures of a dive boat anchored alongside a small uninhabited island with swaying palm trees. That is where I belonged, it was telling me, and for the first two hours I agreed wholeheartedly. My decision apparently made, I felt my failure in finding a transcending practice was telling me that it was not meant to be. So I'll go diving instead.

Funny how the mind works. These thoughts I was having brought out memories of my first backpacking and diving experiences. With a strong desire to go deep into the wilderness, as previously mentioned, I had chosen an area three hundred and fifty miles north of the Arctic Circle in Alaska. Having no equipment nor any idea of what I needed, my first excursion was to the local outdoor equipment and bicycle shop. Well, if there ever was a "they saw me coming" experience, this was it. I left the store with the largest backpack, the biggest and weightiest carrying tent made, and a sleeping bag that needed a stuff sack the size of a hot air balloon. I started out with seventy-four pounds in a backpack that didn't fit me, because it was made to fit a much taller man. As sympathetic as the other very experienced "packers" were, they, with all their juryrigging, couldn't make it fit either. I should also mention that my specially ordered French, never worn, mountain boots were also way too heavy and, of course, a little too big for my feet, even with two pair of woolen socks. I was carrying double of what the books said I should be carrying according to my weight, and five times too much judging by my physical strength and conditioning.

This was, to that point in my life, my most humiliating and humbling experience, and as the genie in Aladdin would say, "I felt very sheepish" throughout the trip. My mind screamed throughout, not a wonderful primal stress relieving scream, but one that comes from deep within a dying ego. I had started out with a brand new everything including an optimistic outlook towards a very male primitive experience, almost to the point of raising my head to the heavens and banging my chest. Thinking that the four women participants would soon fall to pieces and lean on "us" men to help carry some of their loads made me feel even more macho. It was a good thing that we had twenty-three and a half hours of sunlight each day for my war cry of "go ahead and don't worry about me. I'll be in camp just before the sun sets." It proved prophetic more times than not. Physically exhausted and mentally beaten was how I arrived home. It was nearly the same after my first group meditation experience.

Deep sea diving was my next "new" adventure. Here, though, having learned from my experiences with backpacking, I chose a dive instructor who owned his own retail outlet, and I started my lessons towards certification. It wasn't until he certified me that I found out he had never dived in any ocean or sea, just in lakes and rivers in the Midwest. As a matter of fact, he had only been down past thirty-five feet twice since he was certified as an instructor. But what really mattered was that I had in my possession a card that proclaimed me proficient and "certified." Underneath all that bravado was the nagging feeling that I didn't have a clue as to what I was doing or that I was at all competent.

This truly came to the surface sitting on my first dive boat, for it was here I felt I was making a decision of life or possible death. Fortifying myself with my ever present macho ego, I chose to die honorably. Hoping the brown spots on the back of my dive suit weren't noticeable, I stood up, stumbled my way to the boat's edge, and literally fell into the water. Now the one thing I promised myself before leaving for the Virgin Islands was that I would never allow myself to dive beyond sixty feet, for it was at that point where mistakes, if they were to happen, would magnify rapidly. After first allowing myself to be untangled from a surface line by a fellow diver, I was able to descend. The feeling of free falling to the coral below surrounded by bubbles from other divers later became my main reason for trying this a second time. I was so busy trying to remember what to do—to breathe, to adjust the air in my jacket, to keep from banging into the coral, to clear my mask, and feeling slight panic seeing the boat above quickly disappearing—that the first time I remembered to look at my instrumentation I was at seventy-four feet and almost completely out of air. But the funny thing was, I was calm. I swam over to the dive master while calmly giving her the "out of air" signal, and she and I buddy breathed from her tank to the surface. Everyone else arrived at the surface about thirty-five minutes later and proceeded to congratulate me on my maiden dive. The dive master said that not panicking proved that I was a natural, just to keep trying, and to breath more slowly in order to conserve air. Into the water I flopped a second time. This time I lasted about twenty minutes before she brought me to the surface once again. A moral victory, I felt.

Thankfully I had signed up for only two dives and was able to go home with the happy feeling that I had indeed, like Cousteau before me, dived deep within the sea, even though I knew I would most assuredly never do that again. I did though, hundreds of times and with graceful ease, allowing for my human form.

After some time had passed, with each of these experiences I made up my mind that I would train myself both physically and mentally, not only to be able to continue with these adventures, but to develop a high level of skill and competency. The rewards for my decisions were numerous and at times breathtaking. For example, encountering twenty-two bears in a five-day period of backpacking and tenting at the edge of a mountain next to a waterfall that began its long drop to a point thousands of feet below. There were also many exciting dives with sharks, eagle rays, turtles, swimming with schools of tropicals, and joining any variety of angel fish in a quiet "stroll" around a coral head.

Based on my past experiences, it became quite obvious to me that what I needed was more comprehensive knowledge, a better understanding, prac-

chapter two   *Cleansing My Mind*   *12*

tice time, and a greater time frame to make any appropriate decision at all. After all, this was for me a major life decision.

The following Wednesday at 5:30 AM I once again packed my pillows under my arm and with a new resolve headed for the zendo and silence.

~moments came
and went,
where was I?~

~I cannot take even
a moment for
fear of seeing~

~all creation
of itself
itself is~

Chapter Three

*"In silence your heart knows
the secrets of life's mysteries.*

*Why then would you choose
to know in words that which
you already know in your heart?"*

*each step deeper
alters everyday
perceptions........*

chapter three   In Silence

Silence, as I have come to know, is a relative thing, inviting all sorts of vivid thought patterns and magnifying the noises from those around you. A stomach rumble can become an earthquake in progress while a fart transforms itself into an erupting volcano. This is the silence of the zendo, a silence that presents you with the opportunity of great imagination and lengthy conversations with your ego and your nonrhythmic dancing mind.

In the group practicing at the zendo was Dr. Larry Rabin*, a retirement age, tall, imposing, shaved head, twenty-plus years practitioner of Soto Zen. Born and raised in a middle class family in New York City, his formative years through undergraduate school read like a Neil Simon play complete with corn beef on rye and sour pickles "from the barrel at my father's store." A psychology professor who bears the burden of, and seemingly through his own efforts perpetuates, his reputation as a rebellious educator from the 70's. This label he proudly carries daily into the school fray. He is a man who today is obviously a creature of many habits. In the zendo he follows strict procedure and/or ritual, but he nevertheless insists on denying their meaning and importance. This tendency towards denial, I believe, is forced upon him by society's rejection of anyone showing signs of abnormal behavior or thought, and even further,

*The names have been changed.

society's insistence of normalcy and mediocrity. In his position at the university, he carries the usual load of classroom instruction while advising undergraduate, graduate students, and Ph.D. candidates, all this while complaining about the hierarchy, the faculty, and the quality of the students.

On the other hand, he is well published and often reviews the works of top psychologists and the like for prestigious publishers and journals. He brings to the table a Zen attitude and logic that help calm those, me especially, in states of outrageous indignation or turmoil. Having a great sense of humor, he's able to generate a feeling of well-being while imparting his wealth of knowledge to all who will listen. A person once described him as "a man of the mind." For me, his advice and probably more important, his friendship, have been very valuable. I think this Buddha parable best describes Larry's practice: "A man sits rowing his practice boat on the sea. The tide carries him out to a certain point and then carries him back, leaving him once again at the place where he started." As it is with most practices today.

Katherine Sands, on the other hand, is a "woman of the heart." Kindness and compassion layered with a sense of purpose is how I see her. Yet all this splendor, as in a lot of documented cases, springs from a devastating life episode manufactured by

chapter three   *In Silence*   3

her then-husband and father of her children. As the Buddha said, "A beautiful flower can grow from the dirtiest of water." With her children grown, Katherine sought a monastic or community life of spirituality. Traveling far and near she spoke and studied with many groups and people of religion, but in the end she returned to the small city where her need for an inward search took root. Today, she readily admits that she still has not faced and come to grips with her deepest wound, yet recognizes the need to do so. Her "love" is the silence with its pure embrace. She finds that place in her practice with Zen, the Society of Friends (Quakers), in helping others, and traveling with her new pilot husband. A joy to be around.

The supporting cast starts with Dr. and Mrs. Dr. Sanders, clinical psychologists on a restless search. Mrs. Dr. would have fit beautifully in the Paris of the late eighteen and early nineteen hundreds. She is a woman in search of her era and a steadfast clinger to those she chooses to idolize. Mr. Dr. is a man in love with the aesthetics of words. He seems to study and theorize about poetry, books, treatises, and commentaries, but sadly he never becomes one with the meaning of those words.

Besides myself, the present group is made up of four others. Two graduate students, one fragile wounded duck, and a businessman who is into junk, as many who practice to quiet their minds are. These people come to meditate on the average of once a month or less. This leaves Larry, Katherine, and me as the nucleus with the clinical Drs. attending about once a week. An interesting group, but limited in scope because of its numbers.

The only other item of note is our moving the zendo out of the schoolroom into an office suite of one room with no windows. The room was cold and impersonal to begin with, but eventually warmed to the personality of the sitting group. Mainly this move allowed us to leave our cushions and pillows in place and have a permanent altar.

Having read and reread Dogen many times, I found that a peculiar version of his tradition is practiced here. As I was later to learn, most American versions of any Zen tradition are vitiated. Zazen, the practice of silent sitting meditation, the Buddha precepts, the Four Noble Truths, impermanency, and direct experience are the basis for Soto Zen, but at this zendo it was a greatly watered down version. But for me to discuss Soto Zen is a waste of time, energy, and is beside the point. There are literally hundreds, if not thousands, of books on the subject. I will say, however, that a preliminary study of Dogen and possibly Shunryu Suzuki with a touch of Achaan Chah would prove excellent choices for you, as it did me, to gain the background knowledge required to comprehend what I'll be addressing.

As I mentioned before, it was extremely painful for me to sit in the accustomed manner because of the physical problems I created as a youth. This prevented me from paying attention to the workings of my mind, but I was determined to continue. I read somewhere that some martial arts students, as well as most women in the Tibetan tradition, sat to meditate in the kneeling position. Finally able to let go of my "macho" ego, I thought I'd try it for a few days. At the beginning of a second sit after another terrible first attempt, I adjusted my pillow and knelt down. With my butt firmly anchored on the pillow and no pressure anywhere, I was pain free and giddy. Actually a feeling of joy seized me as soon as I settled in, my heart felt like it would explode, and I knew, I just knew that I was going home.

The next few weeks I was feeling light, free, and happy, as I imagine anyone would when his path cleared, and he was able to see or feel the light at the end. But I found myself uncomfortable with the rituals and especially the bowing. I couldn't escape the feeling that I was falling into the religious trappings of multi billions before me and that those trappings would carry me further away from the spiritual dimension I was seeking. So once again I found myself in a lot of pain. It was exactly at this place that Larry and Katherine gave me the most encouragement and solace. Katherine, true to her nature, explained that each person must follow his path, and that all paths lead to the same eventual point. Larry was a rock in his stated view of "do as you must, just have respect for the others and their practice." Of course there was much more along those lines, but basically they patiently allowed me my practice as it was evolving. The mental objectives of Soto Zen were accomplished shortly thereafter, and my transcending beyond began.

After discarding the chains of religions, society, philosophical trash, paradoxes, icons, rituals, etc., and simply opening my mind and heart to achieve that blissful meditative state of unity, my reincarnation awakenings began. These awakened enlightenments revealed to me the true "itness" of who, why and what I am; the itness of all life forms and their natures; and to Universal Nature with its Breath of Universal Life, and their significance. It was further revealed to me the necessity of rebuilding my lost energies and bindings. Almost coincidentally I was awakening to the need for penning the Pure Mind Path in verbiage that would lead humans to the awakening experiences that are essential in order for them to attract a guide for transcendence to an eternal state. Starting now, the percentage of In-Perpetuum Beings in and out of physical form, everywhere, will increase about three-quarters of one percent in the next thousand years or so. Therefore, it is Universal Nature's time to take the historical Buddha's deep awakening to a higher level, with the compassionate hope of awakening humanity to what is beyond, beyond their human nature and their seemingly meaningless lives.

As reincarnates travel deeper inward, reawakening brings about many changes, and slowly they shed the layers of their present life's activities. This affords many surprises; here are two marvelous examples. First, the identities of other human reincarnates were immediately made known to me. To my surprise, some are famous people whom I had read or heard about, but most were people only another awakened reincarnate would recognize. They were revealed to me in varied and sometimes humorous ways. Included were some strange e-mails, phone numbers that appeared while in a meditative state, and words in books that jumbled up and formed names. After awhile I began to solve the mystery of my "hallucinations" and contacted these fellow In-Perpetuum Beings. They proved invaluable in my reawakening efforts, and in my difficult struggle to understand correctly the awakenings I was experiencing. The other was two of the other previous lives I lived.

~In this world of ego and suffering
I melt into a meditative state where I escape
the meaningless activity of
man's mind and actions.

In beautiful isolation I seek
aloneness and silence. It is here I am
afforded a glimpse at the reality of existence,
a glimpse of the simple yet pure Truth.~

~In-Perpetuum Beings:
energy that lights
the universe~

~Tranquil moments—
is this allowable?
Whom do I ask?~

Part Two

Opening Your Spiritual Eye to the Unknown
Identifying the "Hungry Ghost"

There is a purpose and a vision for everything in the universe, humankind is no exception...........

In a Nutshell

Contrary to all known scholarly wisdom, I have asked the summation of this book to be placed at the beginning, not at the end, as would be the case in most literary attempts. I would prefer that you not trudge through these pages only to find that they do not mesh with your preconceptions, therefore you fail to understand the urgent need for one to practice the Pure Mind Way. If you do not comprehend or are unwilling to practice deeply, then Universal Truth, and therefore, this practice, are of no use to you. If you do not, or choose not, to recognize the "hungry ghost" within you that begs for fulfillment, then this book is, again, of no use.

This "ghost" that resides in all humans is the longing that no matter how hard and in how many different ways we try, we cannot quench for any length of time. This is because we are trying to fill a void created by our Universal Nature, rather than one that comes from our human nature. Consequently it is impossible to quench this thirst by performing any logical, emotional, or bodily activity that stems from our human nature. To put an end to this seemingly endless longing and restlessness, we must go beyond our human selves to the spiritual dimensions and experience the true nature of that "hungry ghost." If for any reason whatsoever a practice persists with a lack of deep surrender* and total commitment, it proves out to be useless.

There are five compelling reasons, amongst incalculable others, for humanity to embrace and practice the Pure Mind Way.

First, comprehending with crystal clarity the why, who, and what of all phenomena is achieved by becoming the essence of Universal Nature itself. This state, which is reached by Pure Mind practice, affords us the ability to see clearly through the eyes of Universal Nature. Pure Mind practice accomplishes this by a direct path carrying us through the transcendence of our human nature, our physical and mental limitations, and places us at a point beyond our ego self where we become objective spectators of all physical and spiritual evolutionary causes and events. Only through these eyes can man peer through the "spiritual microscope" and see the realities of all being.

Second, one must attract** and practice under the guidance of an In-Perpetuum teacher for total and

*as defined by me in this record.
**This should not be interpreted as meaning a teacher will tap you on the shoulder and say, "I'm here." For the most part YOU must search, but unfortunately or fortunately, as the case may be, you will find (and they you) many false and delusive people willing to, and many times unknowingly, deceive for their own agendas. Beware of these charlatans and false prophets for it may take years to undo the damage they cause. If you're ready, an In-Perpetuum Being will touch your "soul."

correct comprehension in order to merit the transference of a perpetual energy vessel.

Third, after receiving an energy vessel, it is necessary to continue adding pure energy and to purify all your thoughts and deeds through love, compassion, and kindness.

Fourth, where and how one's dormant energy vessel leaves the body when he passes on will determine whether it will disperse or gather and stay together so that it can be energized. Since the method of its movement and release is not natural to humans at this time in their evolution, it must be learned through extensive practice.

Fifth, a spiritual life practice is the only life worth living for it fulfills humanity's purpose on earth.

You may reject the authenticity of In-Perpetuum Beings or the Pure Mind Path as being too improbable, but if I were to debate it, I would say that due to the limitations of the human mind such improbability is *THE* argument for authenticity.

Although there are many skeletal spiritual systems existing today, virtually all are devoid of their original value. When studied with curiosity towards their practicality of spiritual attainment, they only prove to serve and/or satisfy personal, religious, and communal sentimental and emotional needs. This is true no matter what their own imaginings about spiritual matters may be. After many years of challenged egos, frustration, and the inevitable revisions of their founders' awakenings, these disciplines were discarded by their fervent followers due to the lack of any deep spiritual attainment. Unfortunately these disciplines were carried forward by a few unenlightened beings and are today taught by partially comprehending novices who seek only relief from their human condition and/or financial reward from those who seek Truth. This is true in most Western and Eastern religions.

> ~in a meditative state
> my mind set aside,
> I melt into emptiness.~

Introduction

The Pure Mind Path of spiritual practice is a discipline inspired and driven by Universal Nature so that human beings may transcend appearances and penetrate to the very source of all wisdom. Most of a practitioner's meditative spiritual states are achieved in silent meditation practice, because pure Nature, which lies beyond, yet permeates the nature of humans, resides there.

"Recognizing" the truth of the Pure Mind Path as the Way of generating and sustaining pure energy creating the karmic effect of receiving and/or maintaining an In-Perpetuum state is only a beginning. Recognition and further acceptance for transference of an energy vessel by a mentor (teacher) who is in the state of Perpetual Being and is, therefore, awakened to the deepest level of enlightenment can be a difficult process. One must exhibit and maintain indomitable resolution, willingness to give constant effort, and have developed good concentration as well as restraint. After being accepted by a teacher into a fellowship and/or community of like minds, the whole of the Pure Mind practitioner's (student of awakening through practice) life is seen and lived in non-dualistic form. In turn, practitioners create additional pure energy which is united with, and further harnessed to, the dormant energy vessel in order to maintain that most precious form necessary to become a Perpetual Being.

Awakening teaches us that Truth was first transmitted to human beings during the early stages of their evolution, and that the closer this cycle of form gets to its natural end, the easier it will be for humans to awaken to all Truth. This evolution may take millions of years, so we who live today must practice a very difficult but nevertheless rewarding path if we aspire first to attract and then become an In-Perpetuum Being. This state can only be transferred and maintained while having the mental capacity and potential of the human species. The chance of ever being reborn, anywhere or at anytime, in a similar state is negligible. Realistically, *now* is the only time.

~~Truth;
its seed planted
grows in harmony.~~

There comes a time in a seeker's life when he must end doubt and gain faith. Most people, no matter their success in chasing scholarly degrees or large sums of money or obtaining some degree of intellectual sophistication, whether monk or homemaker, factory worker or physicist, find their hearts filled with pettiness, their lives lacking fulfillment, their minds always doubtful, and their suffering never ending. They are seeking answers to such questions as what happens when we pass on, why we are, who we are, etc. How do we go about negotiating and further eliminating the negative human conditions of suffering and, at the same time, find answers to these time honored questions?

As with most things, it is first necessary to learn the basics; in this case meaning basic morality, seeing the transitoriness of all life, understanding the realities of birth, aging and death, and learning to control one's mind so that it may used correctly. After understanding the true nature of these things, we progress to the transcendent state of freedom from doubt, and gain true faith in the process. As it is in most religious belief systems, study of spiritual texts is not extremely important. Of course, such texts may be wholly correct, but in fact, it is not the ***right way*** to knowing, because it cannot give you right understanding. For example, knowing a person's name is not the same as meeting and getting to know him; the word kiss is not the same as experiencing the act; the printed word hate is not the same as feeling anger, and so on. Only direct and immediate ***experience*** by yourself can instill true faith within you.

There are two kinds of faith. One is based on blind trust of words or in a spiritual prophet guide such as Jesus, Buddha, or Mohammed, or in some religious order which often leads one to practice or ordination. The second is *inner faith*, the certain and unshakable faith which arises from knowing and experiencing from within oneself. Even while awakening to some level of enlightenment, we still have defilements to overcome, and we are best guided by a deeply enlightened teacher. When seeing clearly all things from deep within, we put an end to doubt, suffering, and pettiness and gain faith, thus putting *certainty* into our life and practice.

It is clear to all reincarnates and present day practitioners of the Pure Mind Path and meditation practice that successful understanding and practice presupposes knowledge common to one of the basic Eastern religions or spiritual practices. These include, but are not limited to, Buddhism, Sufism, Zen, or Indian Yogic thought in general, and their well established precepts (in their unadulterated form). Because of the difficulty of Pure Mind practice, it is easier to convey its clearly defined content to those who are in touch with those traditions. Interestingly enough, it was only when Buddhism was transplanted to China and further to Japan that the true understandings and practice traditions degenerated into mere superficialities and word knowledge, as we can easily see from its commentarial literature and comparatively meager results.

This is especially true in the Zen tradition. As it traveled across the waters to the "Western countries" it become more and more an exercise in mental masturbation and frustration. The historical Buddha's awakening was to the immediacy of teaching people the need to awaken, and to the elimination of suffering in *this* lifetime. He taught the clear and indisputable fact of impermanence and the basic morality of compassion. Anything beyond that came from the imagination of past and modern day disciples. These are the same people who receive and give "dharma transmission" without consideration of enlightenment. That differences in viewpoints between the hierarchies in various Buddhist sects arise and persist is not surprising. Buddhist commentaries and sutras are constantly being translated and reflect many different subjective approaches. It is important, therefore, for the seeker/aspirant to be extremely careful in what and who he chooses to read and accept when searching for background material.

Buddhism and Zen can be defined in different ways. Our understanding of those religions is that although Buddhism did not originate as a religion of faith in a transcendent deity (beyond man's limits of experience), it has become one. Initially, it was a religion of awakening to the Universal Nature of oneself. Zen originally aimed to prioritize direct awakening, transmitted apart from any doctrinal teachings, through concentrated practice and mindful living. Instead, it has evolved to reliance on spoken and written words.

The "hungry ghost" focused on in this work is **not** the same "hunger" Buddhists address in their dialogue concerning the human condition of craving or desire. The hunger they speak of stems from man's human nature. Humanity, being a manifestation of the higher Universal Nature, carries that Nature's ravenous desire to know itself. That desire further translates into humanity's deep need to fulfill their reasons for being: first, to quench his "hungry ghost," and in order to accomplish this man must travel beyond himself to know his true Self. Second, to live his life in a way that will attract an In-Perpetuum teacher, and further, to enhance his state of eternal life becoming an energizer of future phenomena. These two important tasks are why we speak of man's need to practice and awaken the Pure Mind Way.

Those who employ metaphors, sutras, another person's awakenings, religious texts, etc. to help satiate their hunger actually increase their emotional state and that very same hunger. Though many millions fall into this category their accomplishments are only just that: an increase in their emotional dependence; nothing more.

introduction 7

To truly satisfy your hunger, stop clinging to the tree trunk created by the religious masses and "go out on a limb, because that's where the fruit is."

The awakening experiences that inform Mahan Agass are of the spiritual dimensions, not religious doctrine, culture or logical mind. Universal Truths cannot be learned from conferences, workshops or books, although they have a place in networking. His embodiment of Truth is an ongoing culmination of awakenings formed by experience and clear perception, not a parroting of words and/or rituals. We also learn directly from awakening experiences by developing the correct tools rather than imitating tradition, and we further embody the integrity of Truth that comes from our uncluttered personal relationship with Universal Nature.

As students we are always willing participants in the realm of learning in order to reach the highest spiritual levels, thereby ending the separation created by mind and ego illusions. These steps involve risks, patience, as well as surrender of our ego desires.

Teachings are not the final destination on our journey. They are the tools to reach clear insight and awareness. ***They are to be used, not collected.***

Affirmation of Truth
manifests in unconditional love.

~wandering the unknown
boynk—
the blind mole learns~

~Tibetan incense rising
through candle's glow—
Truth entwined dreams.~

Ideology

Universal Truths

The following statements are *not formulation beliefs* as can be seen in most religions, but are recognized and known as **Absolute Truth** coming directly from enlightenment communication via the highest spiritual dimensions through the deepest meditative states.

The Pure Mind Practice and its ideology were historically transmitted through a mental bonding between teacher and student while both were in a high spiritual state. From this time on, it will be partially transmitted orally and/or by the written word.

Practitioners of the **Pure Mind Path** know that they know..........

...that any Supreme Being can only be described as Existence itself. Transcending form, space, and time, Existence has no origin, no ending, no self, no face, no emotion, and no direction. Everything that exists exists within Existence. Existence is the only thing that does not depend upon other things for its existence.

....that Existence is energy and if we allow it to flow purposelessly then our lives have no meaning. The fulfillment of our true nature is a matter of becoming, not just a matter of being. It is for each of us to transcend our human nature and condition and become an Eternal Being.

....that Existence's immanent Universal Nature is pure consciousness that flows through all form and space as energy, and as such is known as the Breath of Universal Life; it is this power that guides and dictates the creation of and the natural essence of all phenomena existence.

....that the Breath of Universal Life is the energy that contains, carries, and communicates the essence of Universal Nature, which is the essence of all truth and wisdom that we awaken through our deep meditative practice.

....that Universal Nature, residing in silence, is the nature beyond all other natures including human nature, and permeates all phenomena as their sole and ultimate authority.

....that Universal Nature's laws are just, because they reflect the intricate and dependent nature of all animate and inanimate forms in the universe.

....that the Pure Mind Path is the veritable way leading beyond the ignorance of the human condition to enlightenment and the eternal state of In-Perpetuum Being.

Ideology

....that awakening proves absolutely useless unless manifested in a moral atmosphere of compassion, love, kindness and sensitivity as dictated by Universal Nature.

....that a pure meditative state dissolves the bondage of ignorance. That ignorance is a state of conditioning attributable to man's ego desire, material greed, useless and unfounded teachings, environment, and in all other instances at this time in his evolution.

....that all life is rooted in one existence having a Universal Nature flowing as energy in the twelve spiritual and three physical dimensions of consciousness.

....that our mind and body are the instruments we have to awaken to the Truth of Existence and Universal Nature.

....that energy can be contained and live in three body types: physical form, spiritual dimensions, and polarized vessels, also known as In-Perpetuum or Eternal Beings.

....that In-Perpetuum Beings travel between physical and spiritual planes virtually simultaneously, and that they are the activity of existence and reality itself.

....that the law of karma (cause and effect) has its other side of no-cause/no-effect. Eternal life is an effect and the Pure Mind Path is the cause. Reincarnation is not automatic and must be attained, vigorously maintained, and its movement controlled by living virtuously the Pure Mind Wheel.

....that pure awakening enlightenment comes through a meditative state and must be embodied in our virtuous living and thoughts. That keeping a balanced and healthy mind and body is absolutely necessary to bring forth a meditative state of the highest dimension.

....that beyond the human's nature there is no intrinsic evil, no basis for fear, no ego, no frustration, no desire, no expectation, and therefore, no suffering.

....that the practice of the Pure Mind Path's life wheel creates a total and peaceful harmony of all physical and spiritual dimensions.

Chapter Four

The Pure Mind Path

"From the ego's point of view all
spiritual progress and practice
are one insult after another."
                    unknown

~Awakening petals,
ever floating
through empty space.~

~Moon bathed dewdrops
shackle us
to this world.~

The Pure Mind Path is the spiritual practice enabling one to evolve, through energy transference, into a perpetual state of being/non-being involving the integration of practice, awakening, and embodiment, which liberates one's original self nature. The Path places mind and body in the right motion around a circular wheel that has four main directions of energy creation and flow. They are: downward flow, created by knowledge or understanding; inward flow, created by Pure Mind meditation; outward flow, created by manifestation of the awakenings; and upward flow, created by awakening or enlightenment. There is absolutely no gain to be had unless the Path is lived in an atmosphere comprising the three great positive emotions of compassion, love, and kindness, practiced in a moral way. This morality is conduct that comes from Nature which resides beyond human nature as well as the nature of all other living things, i.e. not killing or abusing nor causing to be killed or abused *any* sentient beings, human or not. These characteristics of conduct are the binding force that holds together the positive energy which we strive to create.

When practiced in total this Path produces enough purified perpetual energy to enable a student to liberate totally his transferred energy vessel from mind/body and further evolve to the state of In-Perpetuum whose primary Universal purpose is the creation of all phenomena. Other than being described as a being in perpetual forms (rebirth is a matter of an individual's choice), he can also be described as having the qualities of being/non-being, thought/non-thought, dimension/non-dimension, timelessness and spacelessness, etc.

The awakening experiences of the Pure Mind Path are a totally personal affair. But it is mandatory to understand that success in attaining liberation, though dependent solely on one's own efforts, also requires an awakened reincarnate's vessel transference and guidance to make it all possible. After awakening through Pure Mind practice, the practitioner evolves to embody those awakenings. Awakenings that do not become a part of one's life practice are, in fact, not awakenings at all, and totally useless.

The most common question asked is, "How, when, and where do I start?" We often reply, "Study, then look carefully and accept where you are in your spirituality, then *quietly sit down!*"*

*See part 3, Q&A for a deeper explanation.

Imitation "seekers" are usually separated out by their unwillingness to undergo the rigors of the zazen meditation practice of silent sitting. If a person is not willing to study and get to know himself through this simple method, the attempt of more advanced methods will place him in peril. Actually it is better if he avoids all metaphysical attempts rather than allow himself to be influenced by energies that will *magnify his fears and faults.* If it were to be said that Zen has a golden truth, it would be its ability to help one understand one's self in order to cure his fears and faults. This removes his ego-driven emotions so that they are not involved in advanced spiritual practice. It also brings with it an effective way of approaching the Pure Mind Path and its advanced practice.

We invariably use the term "walking the path," but it is only a metaphor for embodying the Pure Mind Path and Wheel. "Actually neither you nor the Path/Wheel moves; it is only your mind that moves" (an answer to a Zen koan). When you understand this you will know that you have started.

It may appear to you that the Pure Mind practice places a great deal of emphasis on meditation, mindfulness, and contemplation, but these three channels, though inseparable from each other, form only one piece of the Universal Life Wheel. Together they lead to enlightened awakenings, another part of the wheel, and these awakenings can only be understood by Right Understanding, and they must be manifested by the fourth direction of the wheel, Right Living.

chapter 4   The Pure Mind Path

~:It is a great mistake to judge Pure Mind practice forms of these techniques as being the same as what is being practiced in other disciplines. Outward appearances are not reality.~:~

It has been and will continue to be proven by its rate of successful transcendence that the Pure Mind Path will accomplish more to attract an In-Perpetuum teacher in a much shorter period of time than the practice of Buddhism, Zen, Hindu, or the modern "new age" techniques. The fact is that you can reach states of joy and bliss with Hindu meditations, a state of calmness with Buddhist methods, an ability to function well in the world under Zen guidance, and possibly even relief from symptoms mental and physical that modern Western medicine can't cure. But all these states or gains are illusory when compared to the immortal state reached by transcending the human condition, by going beyond and becoming an eternal being. ~:Our practice is timeless, transcending all forms and is "The Way" as shown by Universal Nature.

The primary difference is that with the other practices you learn "about" things (scholastic knowledge), and you learn "of" it (subjective knowledge), but in Pure Mind practice you learn "in and through" it (inner perception).~:~

The "about" and "of" things are just more layers of knowledge, but through Pure Mind practice you can be permanently transformed. Restlessness in the practitioners of all other forms of "spiritual disciplines" arises as they get a glimpse of something they are trying to reach, but it cannot be attained with these other schools.

Traditional wisdom employed by many religions about their elaborate isolation techniques both long (monasticism) and short term (seven day retreats etc.) is only a process of conditioning to cement and reflect shallow practices and provide mental and physical refuge.

Buddhism in total and Hinduism in part treat meditation solely as a device to make you aware of your real self which is not created by you, but which you already are, and therefore you need not create anything. ~:With Pure Mind you become aware of the need to create, create and bind pure energies in order to become perpetual. Creation of this sort is the first step towards becoming a "creator" of all future phenomena.~:~

~:A highly honed practice of acute awareness is a very important skill and encompasses more than just a momentary noticing of an event or thought. It is the vital and controlling vehicle which puts us in touch with the Breath of Universal Life and the energy of all things. It is the bridge between normal material reality and spiritual reality. This is a skill we are born with, but in a culture stressing strict logic to explain everything in the physical universe, this skill is forgotten and lost to most. Children, in their attempt to master the physical and cultural ways of life, slowly but surely close their door to the spiritual world. Yes, to a certain degree this is necessary so that they may know the difference between the physical and the spiritual worlds.

Much later in human evolution people will focus on the physical world *without* becoming attached to it. Not getting lost in their memory progression, they will be able to go between both the physical and spiritual dimensions without losing touch of either. But until that time, the rebuilding of the bridge to the unknown requires a student to live the Universal Life Path and practice its direction of meditation techniques to accomplish this feat. Acute awareness, or a high state of mindfulness, is required for the attraction and transference of an energy essence vehicle, and that is our aim.~:~

Here are a few important hints that are usually overlooked when one starts into the learning path of meditation techniques. When speaking of reaching the meditative state which allows awakening, one must first know that only the mind which is receptive, here and now, can create this meditative state. Rigidity creates tension, and a tense mind can never be receptive nor meditative. One must, therefore, remain relaxed/weightless and in a non-doing state. Probably the most important thing is to go beyond the paradox that even though our meditations are extremely important, used by us for many critical happenings, we must approach meditation *as such, an end to itself.* Only then can the results we seek be attained.

You must learn and understand the Pure Mind meditation techniques, ~:but in the ultimate sense meditation is not technique; it is acute awareness~:~. When right techniques are used, growth explodes, otherwise you just wander and search and gain nothing. At the beginning meditation seems to be something one does, or a doing, but when one is able to reach a deep state, the doing disappears. The same applies to effort.

With success effort disappears and it's all spontaneous and effortless. You go beyond, you're just there, acutely aware, and it happens; you sit, you dance, you walk, whatever technique you are in, it just happens. With practice you will be capable of leaving effort behind and beginning your inner transformation.

Our minds are intricate, complex, and delicate. If you don't know or understand what to do, it is much better not to do anything, because whatever you do that's wrong creates more problems than it can solve. Don't start unless you fully understand or have a teacher guiding you. Try never to mix two or more techniques, because their functions can be totally different. Sometimes they may even be diametrically opposed. Don't change or try to improve what has been proven successful since the beginning of time. When you don't understand or know, non-doing is more beneficial.

~:Universal Nature is Truth as the Pure Mind Path is the embodiment of that Truth. These Truths cannot be fully understood by ordinary mind nor can awakened enlightenment be successfully communicated verbally, ~:~but we continue to try. If, as with most people, you find that you cannot bring yourself to practice, then at least try to understand the nature of your hungry ghost and live by Universal Nature's moral code in your everyday life ultimately giving it a meaningful existence.

~mindfulness
illuminates
particles of suchness~

Chapter Five

The Universal Life Wheel

"If it is dark enough one candle is plenty."

*Like the food we eat,
meditation practice provides
nourishment as well as heartburn.*

With Pure Mind practice
failure results because you
"do not" not because you
"cannot"....Ooops!..

~:Anything is possible when people set out to reach beyond their logical minds to the spiritual realm. What is impossible is thinking that they can make the rules.~:~

~:The Universal Life Wheel's practice **must be approached as a coherent whole,** not as a way of life that can be comingled with preexisting ideologies.~:~ The problem for most seekers is that they bring with them their culture, religious environment, educational tools, and the need to understand things in a logical way. They thereby view this most spiritual of practices in a conditioned manner. Unfortunately, most Western seekers accept influence by this practice only when a great many of the words and ideas fall in line with their previously accepted ideology. They tend to respond especially to symbols, labels, and titles. It is very difficult for them to realize that In-Perpetuum teachers do not acknowledge certain so-called sacramental or spiritual idols and concepts. These seekers also hold a wide range of assumptions and use a great deal of imagination about what is spiritual and what isn't. What were at one time highly effective spiritual practices are today watered down approximations with meaningless ritual instruments and words. Those who practice these exoteric religions demonstrate by their actions the lack of true inner faith and understanding. Because of modern day superficial and shallow paths to practice, most seekers do not know how to approach a teacher and a teaching as a whole entity. In addition, they fail to understand that they must prepare with the intensity that comes from deep self searching motivated by their "hungry ghost" before they can attract an In-Perpetuum guide for their spiritual life practice. The mystical Islamists use the term "collectors of trifles" for those who seek teachings which fit comfortably in with their accepted pattern or that embody various parts of other teachings which also fit into their ideas of truth or spirituality.

One of the most important qualities a teacher looks for in a prospective student is *his ability and desire to be powerfully influenced without asking why or how it is so.* Humans generally have the commanding desirous ego which needs to control what they believe, or at the least, choose what to accept. This is their ego need to protect all the "truths" of their systems and in turn garner some meaning for their lives. All systems on this earth heavily condition people, and because we do not like to think of ourselves as "conditioned," we say things like "we are dedicated" or very "religious" and we "live" with that explanation. But our brains are engineered to believe whatever the system asks. ~:Man, as a newborn child, has but a few veils, so he is in constant contact with the spiritual dimensions; therefore, Universal Nature is his natural "system" of belief with no questions left to be asked.~:~

Certainty, one of our greatest obsessions, leads us to question everything in order to understand logically, and only when our logical minds are satisfied of something's validity will we accept it as a certainty. This is not a posture that leads to learning, because it sets preconditions, which greatly limit our abilities to go beyond rationality into spiritual dimensions. If you bring certainty as a commanding principle for learning, you bring often tried, failed, and rejected methods, and you will never learn **the essence of what "is."** The other obsession which is a great hindrance is habit-patterns, a form of self-conditioning. Both of these conditions can be bypassed when one goes beyond human nature and awakens to one's true self image and then embodies that reflection. In other words, you are embodying the true "self" and not imitating other people or becoming what they expect. **"Enlightenment eliminates misconception."**

~:The Universal Life Wheel is the practice of living and creating life. It is a living practice that fulfills Universal Nature and thereby our human nature's reason for being.~:~

There are four principle channels (directions) on the path, each having the primary function of creating pure cohesive energy. There are also many secondary channels, but all have the end result of energy production, the difference being in the amount, strength, and polarity. Most disciplines speak of steps along their path, but we only think in terms of breaths. With each breath we take in each and every moment, we seek two things: first, to awaken to Universal Truth; and second, to create the energies necessary to become an eternal being. This Universal Truth is in opposition to most religions and so-called spiritual beliefs. Life is not and should not remain a mystery. Our mission is to awaken and embody its meaning. ~:*Existence is energy and if it flows purposelessly then all life has no meaning.*~:~ The very act of existence is not an achievement; its intrinsic values lie in creation, experiencing, and awakening. Not surprising then, that they are also the intrinsic values of the Universal Life Wheel.

In a high spiritual meditative state you experience the purpose of life. It is at this point that your life becomes freer, free from the mysteries that plague the human, free from the question of life and death, free from the uncertainties of good and evil, and free from the boundaries of the human suffering condition. Here is the point where awakened beings begin to "lighten up" and truly enjoy their lives. They can laugh, sing, dance for no apparent reason. Their weights have been lifted, and they understand that they cannot be judged by the unenlightened masses, and so we find the real meaning of "that crazy monk living on the hill."

~I wanted the truth, so I searched;
I read profusely and listened intensely.
Whether hunger or pain—I overcame;
The others and I we were never the same.

I wanted religion, and so I sought,
meditated with monks many colorful fall,
after time, I knew it not what it ought,
awakened, I understood religion's misguided call.~

~:Spirituality, unadorned, that is the difference. It is the deep inner search that leads to awakening and the embodiment of those awakenings. Universal Nature and therefore its true path, the Pure Mind spiritual practice, ask nothing from seekers but a relationship of **trust and the willingness to allow them to work.** A reincarnated teacher's relationship with a student is one of intimate love, powerful inspiration, and great trust. When the seeker is unwilling in any facet of the relationship, then his ego is in play and it all turns to nonsense. The transformation of a seeker to a student/disciple comes with his willingness to surrender and giving his complete trust unconditionally.~:~

~In a meditative state
beyond the reach of pain;
and still a suggestion of
inexpressible human sorrow
inevitably creeps in.~

It is at this point that we reach the crux of practice and attainment, for the act of surrender is a very decisive step. It's not just a matter of faith in a "Way" but true faith in oneself.

We recognize the act of surrender as a touchy subject with many ambiguous implications. Most people, especially those from Western cultures, have no background or understanding in the relationship between a guide and a student. True faith in one's spiritual practice and its guide demands total trust. This in no way conflicts with statements of accepting only your own awakening experiences as truth. Without "surrender" to a path those deep awakenings will never arise. Those who have experience in awakening might more easily understand.

Surrender cannot take place unless a seeker has total confidence in his decision to do so. A student or disciple gains a cohesive personality because his decision was so monumental and total, so unconditional and absolute. When it comes to Universal Truth and its Pure Mind Path, there are no conditions attached with surrender; therefore, you must first fully understand its practice methods, knowing that you cannot ask for special conditions or bargain for change when embarking on the Universal Life Wheel's course. Our definition of surrender should be interpreted as a letting go of the self; for example, there can be no "if you do..., then I'll comply," etc.

Having totally let go, a student projects this attitude at all times. It becomes obvious to all what his life practice represents. ~:*With surrender a student becomes totally receptive to the Breath of Universal Life and is in communion with Universal Nature.* Awakenings come, and the student/disciple changes. There is almost no possibility that a person may become fully enlightened without a reincarnate teacher. With a teacher, as with the path, a seeker must trust and wholly surrender. The basic requirements must be met in either case.~:~

~The Breath of Universal Life
stands on its own, and never changes.
It can be regarded as the soul of
Universal Nature.

Universal Nature is Truth
and cannot be otherwise.
It is the One
and only thing that does not depend
on other things for its existence.~

~The muted drumming
of a rainy day
disturbs not the silence
nor the thoughts that swarm.

The outside noise
is frantic and shrill
while all within is
quiet and calm.~

Chapter Six

Awaking to the Pure Mind Ideal Through Meditation

*~the final gong.
was it I alone
that knew nothing of it?~*

Meditative state: a transcendence of the normal worldly mind to be conscious through one of the many spiritual dimensions.

If you cannot conceive of the purity beyond the human condition, you cannot come to know inner growth. If you do not surrender your ego, you will be lost and suffer.

chapter 6 — Awakening Through Meditation

Pure Mind practitioners depend solely on the effectiveness of Pure Mind practice, not erroneous beliefs. As it is with other practices, its guidelines do not include impressing upon a student's mind a belief system in place of self awakening. Hearing a teacher or a student say, "I believe this to be true (or is true)" would curl the hair on a true seeker's neck. The "how to" of reaching beyond to the spiritual dimensions is what should be heard. These two ways expressing knowledge and methodology are worlds apart.

There are four primary plus a few secondary considerations for our meditation practice, and each one calls for a different technique, but all play an essential role in our becoming In-Perpetuum Beings. The first purpose is the attraction of a guide or teacher; the second is to satisfy set requirements in order to receive a vessel of purified energies. Third is our creation of the binders that harness this energy vessel; and the fourth is to perfect control and movement of this vessel. Secondary reasons which include the quieting of our minds and living a more productive life are accomplished naturally with the practice.

What then is meditation? Putting it simply, it is ~:"the" door we must go through in order to open our capacities. Meditation is in fact a natural part of our nature, and when we relax ourselves into ourselves, into the very moment, we open and expand our natural capacity for learning, for creativity, for love, and compassion. After a while we come to understand it is our only way to true freedom.

Meditation is "being" in a high state of consciousness and should not be confused with the techniques and methods which are just tools to help transport us there.~:~

Actually there are as many reasons to meditate as there are people who choose to do so. Listed below are a few of the most common ones. Some of these are minor aims, but are a part of our Pure Mind meditation practice, and some results happen naturally simply due to the deep nature of the practice.

~:We meditate in order to attain extraction of self, thereby effecting the freedom of our mind/body. We accomplish this, in part, by mindfulness, which is one way of bringing all the contents of conscious experience into harmony with a common center.

We meditate to be in union with the silence that resides in all form and existed before all form, before all thought, before any gods.

We meditate to understand what our teachers, animals, plants and all of nature have been trying hard to tell us throughout our sentient lives.

We meditate and follow our breath to know our emotions, to understand the emptiness of our ego, so that we may clearly watch the thoughts that arise and fade away.

We meditate because we are at home in pure absolute silence, yet surrounded by sounds of talking, machines, our bodies, and ever busy minds.

We meditate giving up attachments, like pain, for when we let go we give ourselves up and dissolve into silence.~:~

> ~sitting as one
> the ground and I, until
> only the ground remains.~

~:*Freedom,* the ultimate state, allows us just to be ourselves, free from tension and stress, free from worry and suffering, free from the oppressions of the past, free just to be and live fully in the moment of now, and *free from the burdens of sickness and death.* In order to know how to gain back this seemingly lost "freedom" we must first identify the culprit that robs us of that which we prize so highly, "the moments of our life." ~:~Almost everyone looks outside themselves for this culprit and blames whatever is taking place at the moment, whether it be their job, marriage, children, parents, government, "nothing on television," a team losing "the" game or any game for that matter, etc. Our outward search goes on ceaselessly, but ~:*the real culprit, the one that truly robs us of our life is our own out-of-control mind and "it" resides inside.*~:~

Previously we stated that meditation was the door we must go through so that we may open our full potential, but how many asked, "What is the key that opens that door?" Simply put, ~:it is us, in a state as a spectator. This spectator is a detached witness to ourselves, to our body and mind functions, as well as to its relationship to all things. This spectator is our spiritual side which knows who, what, and why we are; this knowledge when awakened allows us to accept ourselves as we truly are, and that is the only true freedom. This freedom from mind allows all other freedoms into our lives. Meditation shows us how to discover this spectator within ourselves. The "door" and the "key" are, of course, metaphors and they should not be considered as separate, because they work simultaneously.~:~

~alive in this moment;
no yesterday,
no tomorrow.~

We may see meditation as a farmer might see the earth; he must first cultivate the earth's soil to prepare it for planting and the growing of crops, whereas we must first construct a perfect frame of mental awareness so that we are instantly ready to absorb what is revealed to us from Universal Nature.

There are many veils that obscure our Universal Nature. The most prominent are: form, ego, will, consciousness, emotions, fear, and dualistic thinking. ~:These veils can only be lifted when seen as non-reality. Our hungry ghosts will be quenched when we know ourselves as not separate but one with Universal Nature in all its physical forms.

In a high state of consciousness we come to know how wondrous we can be and fully realize that only in our mind/body do we have the ability to attract a teacher to "become" the perpetual spiritual and physical energy that gives life and light to all.

We are fully expressed when we advance inward to an awakening of completeness, and we actualize that in the way we think and live.~.~ The catch 22 is, in order to reach that awakening of completeness we must first live and think that way. We must either start with or eventually come to Pure Mind meditation.

Silent Sitting Techniques

Practically speaking we are unable to control our minds, because to a very large extent we are not able to concentrate. In reality we are not able to do anything of our own volition (especially in the spiritual realm), and we are therefore dependent upon other people and the environment to stimulate us in new ways so we can maintain interest in our daily lives. **Can you imagine?** We desperately need other people to prove our lives worthwhile. Unthinkable to those having attained a high spirituality.

~:With time, silent sitting will overcome the distractions and restlessness. Concentration, con- trol and contemplation naturally follow forcing our lives into transformation at the deepest levels.~:~

Lesser practices, religions and disciplines, though saying otherwise, confuse meditation techniques with meditative states and in some cases enlightenment. Those teachings and guides (gurus, dharma heirs, priests, etc.) who speak of the means as the desired end result are false and useless and should be avoided at all costs. Actually it is because most practices can only take you to a certain point along the "way" that they preach *that point* as the objective and call it an enlightened state. Meditation methods, techniques, and disciplines are the "how" not the why.

Pure Mind Techniques for Silent Sitting

> "We sit in silence
> to be where thinking
> has not yet started."
>
> _{unknown}

In our seated meditation practice the positioning of the body is of vital importance, best described by T.K.V. Desikachar as "steady and firm yet gentle and soft." The two primary points are a straight back and a low center of gravity. In order to support the back we use a cushion or pillow and preferably a mat. Our goals here are to insure that the natural curve of our spine does its work and that we are solidly in contact with the ground.

After sitting down place your legs in your position of choice (see below), raise your buttocks off the cushion and push them back. You can easily accomplish this by leaning forward and placing your hands palm down in front of your knees, then sitting back with your pelvis forward and buttocks raised. When you are properly seated, your center of gravity will be at the point at which all of the forces at work in the body will naturally meet. A straight back is needed to accomplish this. At first this may seem unnatural, but after a time it will become apparent that this is our body's natural posture. For most, in the beginning this posture is difficult, but for the long haul it is, by far, the one that works the best. The physical body will feel rigid at the beginning, but actually we are very much at ease and totally relaxed. It takes a lot of "pillow time" practice to rid yourself of pain and restlessness.

Your legs can be placed in any of the three popular lotus postures or its Burmese variation. The kneeling postures popular with the practice of the martial arts are also excellent. As with the lotus, in kneeling we also use a cushion, either by placing it across the legs on the calves and sitting down, or straddling it so there is no pressure on legs or feet. All of these time tested methods, and more, can be found in many books at your library under meditation or yoga, etc.

No matter the seated posture, the position of the head and back remain the same. To put your head in the correct position, pull your neck up as if trying to touch the ceiling with the top of your head which automatically drops your chin to its proper position.

The positioning of your eyes and lids depends upon the meditation technique that's being attempted. With the simple silent sitting technique you can either keep your lids slightly open with your eyes unfocused or lightly closed, depending upon which better allows you to stay acutely alert. Then again, there is the "third eye" technique which calls for focusing your eyes. As you learn and experiment with the possibilities you learn which works best for you.

The positioning of the hands is also dependent upon the meditation technique. In all energy movement meditations the hands should be placed with the right hand resting open, palm up, fingers pointed left and the left hand resting upon the right, with the middle knuckles touching. The thumbs should touch ever so lightly forming a beautiful oval. There is a lot expressed and communicated in the way hands are held and how they touch. This method is preferred in silent sitting and/or energy creation, but not mandatory.

Using a chair to sit if one is incapable of getting into or maintaining the other positions is acceptable, but will not be of help in energy movement meditations, for which you must be on the ground. Actually lying down on the ground is better than sitting on a chair for those techniques. If you sit in a chair, do not rest your back, and use a firm chair that's the correct height for your legs to rest comfortably on the floor.

Our minds have important functions in all our meditations. Foremost are: the creation of pure energy, visualization through imagination (a part of that creating process), contemplation, interpreting the awakening experiences, and the seeking of the Breath of Universal Life which is the transmitter of Universal Truths. Of course a mindful state is necessarily always present. ~:Done correctly, some meditations have a way of breaking up the walls in the mind and further softening the heart, helping to fulfill our purpose.~:~

~:A few thoughts about the difficult topic of contemplation. Using words in an attempt to examine and explain the contemplative state is frustrating. For example, contemplation can be called a passive state, but at the same time it is intensely active. It is a state without an object center; therefore we have nothing to concentrate on, yet it has all the intensity of deep concentration. It has no thought process, yet it is called by some, meditation. It is a state where, if we were trying to accomplish anything, it would be awareness without attachment (reflection). It is knowing without a subject who knows, or an object that is known. *Although this state, some say, is very remote and even inaccessible, the constant and devoted practice of the Pure Mind Path will allow this state to reveal itself, slowly at first, but with ever increasing surety.*~:~

There are as many varied tools as there are "paths" that have been forged over the centuries to help us reach a meditative (contemplative) state while sitting. Thus there is counting the breath, watching the breath, feeling the breath, watching the rising and lowering of the diaphragm as we breathe, controlling the breath, not controlling the breath, on and on. Then, too, there are all those other techniques like dancing, humming, sexual contact, whirling. What must be understood is that there are different means for whatever you are trying to accomplish. On the Pure Mind Path we must accomplish many different things, and we reside in many different states, in and out of physical forms. So the tools of meditation change with the aim. It would be foolish to think that they all work in all cases (or any for that matter), and most are dependent upon the makeup of the individual who is attempting their use. The correct tools used for our practice are described throughout this text starting with third eye meditation. ~:Non-attachment of thoughts and emotions that arise stemming from the constant input of the senses and remembering to "just let go" are crucial.~:~

~On my sitting pillow
I lay aside the dark recesses
of my tortured human mind.

There where silence is spawned
I flow beyond to the spiritual
dimensions of pure white light.
In this realm where all natures
transcend their separateness,
I find myself at home, once more.~

Deep Third Eye Meditation

~:There are three very important factors in Pure Mind third eye meditation: recognizing our third eye, the role of ourselves as a spectator, and acute awareness or attentiveness. This meditation method is both highly dynamic and calmingly passive at the same time. It thereby allows pure energies to be created while a quieting of the mind takes place which creates the opportunity for awakening experiences to arise naturally.~:~ Some also believe that in this technique lies the key to unlocking the spiritual dimensions so highly sought. To the Tibetans, Buddhists, and Hindus the third eye plays a very important role, and to the mystics of most Asian practices it is the window "beyond."

The pineal gland, science tells us, lies between our two eyebrows and is said by scientists to be the most mysterious part in our bodies. Here also resides our third eye, but to the ordinary person it is only imaginary, something out of fairy tales, myths, and the mysterious Orient. To mystics and Eastern practitioners the "third eye" and this mysterious gland are known to be one and the same.

~:Normally in a non-functioning state, the third eye awaits our evolutionary process to go beyond our "now" selves and become active. Fortunately, it can be opened by simple methods, but it takes knowledge of its existence, patience, and a lot of practice to do so.~:~ We find that, dependent on the individual, there are slightly different ways of "finding" our third eye, but all methods can work equally well. This depends on the person.

Sit on your pillow as you would in your silent sitting posture with hands placed in the energy mudra. Take a few very deep breaths Kriya Yoga style, then focus your eyes on the very tip of your nose. Do not strain, just allow them to rest there and gently stare. Keep your attention there as long as possible, again without straining your eyes. Your eyes will, after a while, naturally come to rest at the correct place. Then slowly drop your lids so that you can see the tip of your nose though a very thin crack. When the eyes are correctly placed there is an attraction, a magnetic drawing, so to speak, from your third eye which starts to take you in. It is here from "inside" the third eye that you begin to see the outside relative world in a single, non-dualistic mode of awareness. You see as a spectator.

Starting with such attentiveness, the third eye leads you to the freedom of seeing things in terms of their "itness" or "isness" instead of as a composition of aggregates, and having attained a clear, quiet mind you develop a state of acute awareness. This state evokes the Breath of Universal Life with its knowledge energies, and we begin to experience the awakening process.

The old mystical scriptures speak of deep attentive awareness as the means of opening the third eye. This method which brings a concentrated effort to the gland itself will bring it out of its coma. Probably for the first time you will experience the seeing of thoughts racing in front of you and not "inside your head." It is here and now that you are the spectator, not the player of mental pinball. All our lives we are what we think, we are the players and therefore the game itself, but in this phenomenal state we are the observers, the witnesses, the spectators. It is here that we can observe our pains, our physical and mental suffering, understand from whence they come, and how, in fact, they have no identity, no life, unless we give it to them by identifying with and attaching ourselves to them.

The paradoxical question of "if you become a spectator, then who is watching you, the *spectator*" is answered simply: ~:the third eye is the spectator, and you, by seeing solely through this third eye become as one "the spectator" itself.~:~ These happenings, as always, must be experienced; they cannot be judged by outsiders or understood with words. The difference between this method and those that just concentrate on feeling and/or counting the breath is that instead of using our time solely with concentration exercises that allow us to see things a little clearer than we normally see them, by opening the third eye we see beyond our breathing and breath, and we can actually know the breath's essence, or the breath within the breath, the Breath of Universal Life. We can feel its energy, see its form, know its nature, and experience a true living joy. **It is here that you stand poised and awakenings come. It happens. We know, and so can you!**

A slightly different approach calls for the eyes to be completely but lightly closed. Follow the previous instructions, but as you are dropping your lids, pause for a moment to focus on the tip of your nose, then continue dropping them until they are closed. In either case stay with this meditation for as long as it takes to find the correct position of the eyes, to allow the third eye to awaken and to evoke the Breath of Universal Life. Always keep in mind that awakened energies are, by far, the most powerful and the purest. When you add the joy to the love in awakening it's like building your new sailboat with the best wood, perfect plans and strong nails.

Energy Movement and Imagination

The spine plays a very important part as a base for both your body and mind. For our purposes let us say that there are five centers or energy pockets along the spinal column*. One end is the very top of your head and the other is at the sex center. The middle three are located between those two; one is at the navel, one is alongside your heart, and one is at your third eye gland. In one of the following techniques the purpose is to gather your energies and send them down deep into the earth creating an attracting energy cylinder for the earth's very powerful energies to flow up into your body and mind.

*Actually there are seven following the spine upward and seven below.

One of the most important understandings of energy movement is that willpower, desire, needs, and the like will not move energy. We must first learn to move our energies by imagination. We have been led to believe that imagination is a cerebral activity and therefore useless in everyday life realities, when in fact imagination is much more in its relation to spirituality. ~:Imagination is an actual vehicle that helps carry Pure Mind students to unknown spiritual realms or dimensions. Thought and feeling energies aid in strengthening our imagination.~:~

What is imagination? On one hand, our power to imagine seems to be illogical and irrational, yet it is our imagination that helps us realize our greatest dreams. The greatest accomplishments of technology, music, art, and discovery began with creative images that were conceived in the realm of imagination. We remain skeptical, because we are taught that the imagination creates illusions, but we admire its unending creativity. We are extremely uncomfortable with our fear of not being able to control it, yet we are fascinated by the possibilities it offers us. We doubt its use in the face of logic, but we wish we had more of it. We feel that somehow imagination goes the way of childhood, lost forever, but in fact it's just buried beneath layers of social conditioning. Practicality, not imagination, is supposed to enable an economically stressed society to function. For example, anything beyond using your imagination to avoid traffic in order to get to work on time, or how to attract a partner for sexual stimulation and/or procreation might be considered by some as insane and taboo.

~:For the student of Pure Mind meditation, imagination means more than mental masturbation; it is a vital and primary vehicle, because it helps connect us with the Breath of Universal Life and with the energies in all things.

Using imagination skills requires breaking the walls we raised in our attempts to master the physical and cultural ways of modern life. This must be accomplished so that we may reestablish the bond between the physical and the spiritual worlds.

The means we have of creating a line of communication with the world of energy is critical in attracting a guide and later maintaining an eternal state. That eternal state exists as a vehicle of our natural pure energies, combining with energies we have attracted, bound together with the energies we created by our embodiment of love, kindness, compassion, and it's sprinkled with our untainted personality traits.~:~

We use imagination to visualize what exactly we are trying to create or have happen. It is a manipulation of thoughts and feelings to create a visual and/or sense-oriented image to that end. We do this by:
1: Creating a mental image of an exact experience we want to happen.
2: Defining it in great detail.

3: Gathering our energies from all our centers and sending them to our sex base.
4: Infusing the image with energies we have gathered at our sex base, creating and adding further excitement and enthusiasm energies.
5: We continue to add strength with our emotions and senses. If we lose it, we start again.

This method is totally interactive with the environment, the Breath of Universal Life and Universal Nature. It is, therefore, very powerful and creates a lot of action. What you're doing is mobilizing your energy's forces and, through the power of your mind and emotions, sending them out to intercede and communicate with all other energies that exist both in this world and beyond. Understand that you don't always control the events that you experience, but you do control your responses. The more active your imagination, the more powerful you are and the greater the volume of energies attracted for your energy vehicle. To be successful is to break down the walls between the world of ordinary reality and the spiritual dimensions.

Imagineering can be slowly relearned by walled-in humans. One small step at a time, successfully completed, and you may find yourself sitting on a cloud enjoying a view of this earth.

Be successful in each task before moving on to the next. Do not combine the exercises unless it is called for.

Awakening Your Senses

All our senses must be used for creating images and infusing them with "life." Since our goal is to have our imaginary creations, experiences, and forms transformed into reality, we must fully develop all of the following techniques to their optimum.

#1 Technique
Should be continually practiced outdoors as well as indoors.

Close your eyes and breathe deeply. Relax, touch, smell, and listen to the things immediately around you; get to know each intimately. Do each of these things seeking depth of knowing.

Then combine the three sensations and allow them to flow inward.

#2 Technique
Choose five different objects, one for each one of your senses.

Look carefully at your chosen sight object, then

close your eyes, breathe deeply and relax, then recreate it in your mind to its finest detail.

Physically pick up and feel your chosen object, then close your eyes again, breathe deeply, relax, put it down; recreate the feelings you got from it.

Continue to do these exercises for smell, taste, and sound, making sure you can successfully recreate each with your imagination dimension.

These exercises should be practiced outdoors as well as in, taking but a short amount of time for each. You must continually be successful, each and every time, before moving on.

#3 Technique
Having successfully completed techniques one and two many times, we move on to recall and recreation.

Sit or lie down comfortably. Close your eyes, breathe deeply and relax yourself. Choose an object that you have become very familiar with, picture its shape, then change everything about it. For example: recalling an apple, stretch it out so that it has the shape of a banana, and if the original apple was smooth to your touch, feel it as furry; taste it as a peach and give it the odor of your wet dog; and finally, hear it speak to you as your sister.

These exercises might seem simple and a little childish, but they are very, very important, because they stimulate your imagination back into detailed use and enable you to create, recreate, and empower these creations with energy and therefore life. It is a beginning step for the human to fulfill Universal Nature's design.

Gathering Pure Energies and Eliminating the Tainted

Systematized Technique for Gathering and Assimilating Earth's Pure Energy

1: Assume your chosen position for silent sitting, with one exception. If you normally sit in a chair find a way to sit on the ground, even if you must stack a lot of pillows and need help getting up and down.

2: Take three to five very deep breaths using the diaphragm, not the chest.

3: Start gathering your energies from the center at the top of your head, and continue down collecting from all the centers and holding the energies at your sex center.

4: Using the methods outlined for visualization by imagination, create the image of you as a cylindrical energy vehicle that will be transported to the center of the earth. You do not ride this vehicle because you are the vehicle.

5: Take yourself down, observing, feeling, and listening all the while to earth's energies.

6: When you reach the earth's hot core, picture the energy anchored, and slowly return your mind to your body.

7: The energies of the environment will follow your cylinder up into your mind/body. Hold them there with soft loving thoughts, thereby binding them to you.

8: Come back to physical reality very slowly and gently.

~:These energies that are now a part of you contain the wisdom of our earth's nature and become awakenings for you to understand, embody and manifest. If you do not bind them, they return to the environment from which they came, and you have gained nothing except an experience.~:~

Because energies, in part, are created by emotion and thought, they have color. Look carefully and you'll see.

With the seeker's mind cultivated by the changes brought about by the simple meditation techniques we have discussed, he may now be termed a student. Although not very far on his path, he is at least prepared to advance at a greater rate. At this point he has to a great degree learned how to still his mind and overcome his physical restlessness. He would have touched and been touched by energies and awakenings from beyond his everyday consciousness.

The meditation techniques outlined in this record are a prerequisite for the advanced and specialty techniques of the kind that should only be learned and practiced under the tutelage of an In-Perpetuum Being or a recognized advanced disciple. These advanced techniques have evolved from the beginning of man's awakening and are, for the most part, kept secret. This is to protect the individual practitioner from the misuse of power- ful energies. They are not divulged until the teacher knows beyond a doubt the goodness and compassion of the student's heart and that his motives are pure. Modern education conditioning, the economic drive underlying our present day focus, and the sciences having revealed many truths and created many conveniences, have nevertheless inhibited our ability, understanding, and appreciation of the spiritual dimensions and the methodology to attain them. Building a practice is like building a seven layer cake. The first few layers are sturdy and deep for they must carry the rest. Therefore none of the lower layers or meditation techniques can be abandoned as a student rises to build the top layers.

Sometimes the practitioner brings to bear all or some of the techniques at once, other times he selects the one most suited at that moment. To outsiders who are unfamiliar with the origin of the practice and are also incapable of grasping abstract concepts, our practice's techniques are viewed as a confused hodgepodge of meditations and mystical states. But as many practitioners from other disciplines will tell you, logical thought is actually one of the great barriers to spiritual attainment.

With the preliminaries behind him, the student has transformed into a being apart, dedicated to the Pure Mind Path of attainment for the sake of becoming an Eternal Being. As with most things, his accomplishments towards that end will depend upon the situation he finds, or has placed himself in. If the student is living a monastic existence with his practice as his life, he will move rather quickly. Laymen with other responsibilities will have to do the best they can, and they most of all will need a lot of guidance and patience as they try to juggle their "normal" life with the spiritual. For those few who gain the courage to live the Pure Mind Wheel as their life, their ideal situation is to live as a full time resident of a Pure Mind community apart from society, thereby renouncing the worldly life. Some, however, choose to live totally as a hermit monk.

> ~On my cushion sitting quietly
> all my restlessness stills,
> like circles on water it too fades away.
>
> My burdens lie where they lie,
> where I left them,
> adrift in their own way.
>
> Fear rises. I enter into my fear,
> become my fear, then what I fear
> from my fear leaves me,
> soon my fear of it evaporates.
>
> With my fear's dying moan
> my ego lets go and
> my heart joyfully opens.~

Chapter Seven

Our Living Practice

*"If you do not get it from yourself,
where will you look for it?"*

~buried in
spiritual essence:
experience to live.~

~anxiety is nonsense!
spring peppers call to me;
keep on sitting,
in summer's heat,
in winter's chilling.~

chapter 7 — Our Living Practice

~:Our embodiment of Universal Nature's moral code, fulfillment of our need to awaken, to define, to adjust evolutionary paths, and to energize latent possibilities are the aims of Pure Mind practice and is, in part, the practice itself. Whether one is awakening or reawakening does not matter; the practice remains the same. The Pure Mind practice to become an eternal being is the only true path fulfilling humanity's life purpose. It does this by taking us beyond the limited expectations of our human body/mind nature to spiritual dimensions where we gather and bind pure undefiled energies to attract and secure an energy vessel. This is the highest possible aim of any human and, therefore, the practice should be taken up in a mental attitude befitting such a high purpose.~:~

~:Keeping in mind the true significance of an In-Perpetuum Being, that of a creator of future phenomena working hand in hand with Universal Nature, instills confidence in the student. This confidence begins with awakening to the pure and gentle heart of Universal Nature through its Breath of Life and is important for the meditative process. Once a student totally surrenders to the Pure Mind Life Wheel and his teacher, he relaxes into a meditative and an acutely aware life. Having learned the definitive purpose of life, he acquires a great deal of conviction which fills him with further ther confidence and joy. Awakening to his capacity inspires a determined attitude to attain the deepest enlightenment and reach the highest spiritual state. Surrender, recognition and relaxation are the prime movers. Surrendering the ego in favor of a blissful union with Universal Nature unlocks the natural energy channels and truth flows unhindered.~:~

>~Surrendering all;
>union
>becomes us.~

In one way Pure Mind practice is very strict, because the time of its practice is the whole day every day, and the place of practice is anywhere and everywhere. We are, of course, speaking of our embodying and manifesting Universal morality and codes. Together with a high state of mindfulness, this is how a student conducts his activities throughout all his life. A program of Pure Mind meditation practice, on the other hand, depends on the circumstances the student finds himself in. A seeker or student living outside a spiritual community should, when beginning, hold formal meditation sessions a minimum of twice a day. The first one should end somewhere between the first light of the dawn and about fifteen minutes after the sun breaks the horizon. The evening session should be held between dusk and before lying down to sleep. An additional session of something between twenty and forty minutes just before eating lunch is highly recommended. It is much better if you do not eat before any session. Living in a community the student simply follows the guidelines set down.

Morning meditation can take one of three forms. Three forty-minute meditations with two ten-minute breaks in-between, or a single one-hour meditation, or two forty-minute meditations with one ten-minute break between. The choice is up to the individual depending upon his circumstances, ability to sit for long periods, and his state of advancement. Since we have two different aims for meditation, there are different methods. First there are the awakening meditative methods. Secondly there are the energy creation and gathering methods. In the case of beginners, silent sitting is the one and only practice. Until a student conquers all restlessness and pain becoming totally relaxed within the sitting position, he should not move beyond. The silent sitting position he adopts will be the basic position for most of the advanced methods, so he must be totally at ease and able to sustain it for long periods of time. Using one of the breathing methods for concentration is perfectly all right at this point. These age-old exercises can help take the mind off any physical pain, and also help some students calm their minds. Restlessness and pain are not unusual, and will dissipate in the course of diligent practice. For more information and procedures in silent sitting practice (Zazen) beyond those described in the meditation chapter of this record, choose any Zen Buddhist instruction book and follow its methods. But remember to cross-reference with Pure Mind methods and most assuredly your guide/teacher. Bringing yourself to a point where you're able to advance may take anywhere from one to three years, dependent upon your physical and mental conditioning when you begin, and how you progress.

Even when practiced in a group, meditation is a wholly personal experience. There are certain dynamics that take place as part of a group, but within those dynamics it's the personal experience that sanctions one's movement. You, therefore, should not allow yourself to become irritated, annoyed, or discouraged by the disruptive behaviors of others. Zen and Buddhist teachings state that we should take all these things, including our personal disturbing thoughts, as temporary and should see them as part of our practice. This distraction of one's state of mind, they claim, should be made an object of contemplation. This might be fine for those whose sole purpose has become, or was originally, that of connecting meditation experiences to the understanding and living of their ordinary lives, but for us whose life and practice has a further purpose this becomes unacceptable and should be eliminated. Contrary to Buddhist teachings, when dealing with these types of interruptions it is "lost time."

Within our Pure Mind practice, disturbances are a waste of our precious meditation, living, and/or working time, and we cannot afford nor should we have to deal with the transforming of these into useful objects. We must allow ourselves and be allowed to keep to the primary subject of our meditation and object of our lives.

The beginning student's day consists of meditation periods morning and night (and at noon when possible) with awareness and mindfulness consistently practiced throughout the day. Thinking thoughts and performing deeds of love and compassion, being kind and sensitive should be practiced throughout all of our moments.

Advancing, the student adds the practice of imagineering techniques wherever and whenever he can find ten to fifteen minutes to do so. These are fun and since the freedom to have fun is a true by-product of our practice, we do a lot of lying on the ground, imagining with the clouds.

These techniques should be perfected before moving on to the energy creation and attraction meditation methods. If the basics are not perfected, advancing on to these other techniques would be a waste of time.

Until sitting on your pillow becomes second nature

with none of the usual distractions, a student should not attempt the powerful "third eye" meditation. When a student is ready, this meditation can replace silent sitting. When first beginning, however, it is acceptable to switch back and forth between the two until there is no eye strain during the third eye technique.

The secondary training methods of silent sitting and imagineering are the foundation and building blocks for the rest of our meditation techniques and are retained and utilized throughout a practitioner's entire life. These seemingly simple exercises, when given persistent practice, will gradually lead to the highest results. The main emphasis rests with the creation and movement of energy.

Altars, idols, and various paraphernalia used throughout religious communities are for the most part considered meaningless within this practice. ~:If one feels the need of these things to help motivate or maintain one's discipline and practice, Pure Mind living would be useless. The motivation to continue practice is strictly in its direct results. Without such inner faith, through recognition of its aim, one should not even begin, for the results besides being useless, could also be detrimental.~:~

We typically use a low table on which sits a vase

with an imitation silk flower and buds symbolizing the continuing flow of life, a candle symbolizing the light of awakening, and an incense holder, because incense helps us create an atmosphere conducive to reaching the spiritual dimensions. We sometimes use a gong to start and end individual meditations. When in a group it announces "quiet time" and when alone it aids in centering our attention.

Bowing, though important to most other practices for reasons we cannot yet fathom, is not called for by Universal Nature or in the Pure Mind practice, with one exception, and that is, at the very end of a session. While still seated on our pillows we bow to each other in recognition of the many, many things that we should honor in each other, including effort, friendship, community, and trust. Though very meaningful we regrettably neglect to acknowledge these people otherwise.

The reading aloud of scriptures, sutras, and the Bible, etc. is an important part of all worldly religions, but again, not this practice. These readings were welcomed and necessary in the days when seekers and practitioners were uneducated; they needed the repetitious droning of spoken words to learn the "why and who" of their respective religions. It is still insisted upon today by hierarchy and teachers seeking resources for purpose, motivation, and emotional highs otherwise easily lost within their flock.

In this practice we do nothing to stand out, absolutely nothing to set us apart. Religions and spiritual practices that bestow titles, robes of position, and various other artifacts should be scrutinized for the egotistical and/or control factors that are supported by this type of habitual foolishness. This is especially true for those practices that teach the unity of all things, but nevertheless impose separation and status hierarchies. Teachers should be judged by their deeds and presence, not by their rank or what they say, wear, or write.

Among us, a student may choose to address his guide/teacher in whatever way is comfortable for him and is acceptable to the teacher. There are no "correct" titles, no "reverends" or "roshis." We have no priests to perform weddings or funerals or rites of passage. A reincarnate may carry or have objects from his past lives, and some have replicas of some former dress, but this is in private or at a formal meditation session, never in public or as an ego symbol of attainment or appointment. An Eternal Perpetuum Being knows who and what he is and needs no outside recognition to validate his existence. Actually we seek anonymity, because it helps Universal Nature's aim and our practice.

Living and working conditions in any city make it difficult to maintain sustained periods of strict practice. Even though a serious, persistent practitioner may sometimes get good results, his progress will be very slow and difficult. Attracting and maintaining a state of In-Perpetuum, most times, depends upon a regular strict practice with constant monitoring by a guide. Progress is in direct relation to beneficial practice conducive to energy creation. You can extend your daily practice by bringing your mind to mindfulness during any activity. Not only will this help your practice, but it will aid in obtaining better results in your work. Furthermore, by replacing social contact with practice during private hours, one finds more productive and creative opportunities.

There is no set way to dress for meditation sessions, but it is highly recommended that both males and females wear simple dark, preferably black or dark blue, tops and pants. No low cut tee shirts, shorts, dresses or skirts, except those that fall to the ankle while standing or are covered by a shawl, wrap or robe. Shoes and hats should never be worn at a session, but dark socks and shawls on cold days are fine.

Silence is mandatory from the moment one rises (except in an emergency) until the very end of the first session.

Any exercises one chooses to perform must be completed by the first bell. A lot of practitioners like to stretch their necks and backs at their pillows, some like to include breathing exercises; this is up to the individual.

Kinhin (Zen walking meditation) is not a part of this practice. One just stretches or walks in silence between meditations. Always be back at your pillow one or two minutes before the first bell.

After lighting a candle and incense stick, you may formally start (and end) each individual sit with four bells as a reminder of the four prime directions of the Universal Life Wheel.

When the bells start ringing, place your tongue on your palate just behind your front teeth. It should remain there for the whole meditation. Then take a few deep breaths and settle deeply in your posture. A slight rocking side to side may help your balance before settling in. Make any adjustments to your posture, when necessary, slowly and quietly, being very mindful of the others.

Example of an individual's daily practice program: Normally six or seven days a week

5:30-7:00 AM   two 40-minute silent periods
                     or one 60-minute silent period

chapter 7   Our Living Practice

11:30 AM   20 to 40 minutes in silence
           (20 min. is minimum for any sit)
5:30-6:10 PM one 40-minute silent period
           yoga practice once a day
Three-day session normally on a weekend:
Friday and Saturday (fall & winter)
   5:00-8:00 AM silent meditations
   8:00-9:00 coffee and breakfast
   9:00-Noon work
   Noon-1PM lunch
   1:00-2:30 PM work and personal time
   2:30-4:00 PM meditation
   4:00-5:00 PM discussion, chanting, music etc
Sunday: 5:00-8:00AM silent meditation
End of session—The meditation hall remains open until 4 PM Friday and Saturday.

Most aspirants, due to their social conditioning, are incapable of comprehending and forming a deep spiritual, ego defying practice. They therefore exclude themselves from becoming students. Many have the potential to attain, but they do not appreciate that the methods are important, and very few have learned how to approach the problem of going beyond their mind's limitations to awaken (partly because they do not recognize their mind as a problem). Being a student means going beyond wanting to learn, by knowing that how to learn is a learned ability. Desire is not enough. Sincerity, willingness, surrender, and wonder are the basis for learning.

If you adopt the Pure Mind Wheel as your life practice, then you will find yourself observing yourself. If you practice with the idea of being one way or another, it will be useless, especially during meditation. You cannot bring expectations or your own ideas to your pillow. All your intellect and opinions should be left behind so that every moment you practice, in any one of its forms or methods, you are there, completely empty.

"The more talking and thinking, the farther from the truth." Seng ts'an

~Morning Meditation

Down the hall
through curtained windows
dissolving moonbeams
reveal a worn
black cushion.

A match is struck
exposing a lone dark figure;
candle and incense
will burn till dawn.
Sitting in unity
with a mind so clear
the (energy) waves carry me
across the galaxies
well beyond man's understanding;

> it's here the ancients greet me
> as they mystically appear.~

Pure Mind practitioners are constantly reminded to make themselves familiar with the other aspects of life that can form a link of understanding to what exists between themselves and Universal Nature. Some of these aspects are: food, drink, drugs, minerals, dance, singing or chanting, music, relationships both sexual and non, productive work, exercise, and the air that enters our bodies. These things, especially those that we ingest, if not in harmony with human nature's intent, transform man from animal to lesser animal, instead of animal to man.

With students of spirituality, foreign, toxic, and harmful things which create a diseased body and mind prevent them from any chance of rising beyond to the spiritual realms of Universal Nature's Ultimate Truth and becoming an In-Perpetuum Being.

The test which is consistently placed in man's way is to separate what is nutritious and healthy from those things he has been conditioned by society to ingest, and this includes his own hedonistic appetites. If a student chooses not to confront and question the erroneous propaganda about his physical and mental wellbeing that an economically driven

chapter 7   *Our Living Practice*   14

society bombards him with, he places his practice, as well as himself, in constant physical and mental peril.

Students of the Pure Mind Path reach a point in their practice where they realize their ignorance in attaining the physical and mental balances that must be achieved in order for them to rise above their present spiritual state. Turning their thinking to the basic Truth of an existing natural order, they are able to separate their conditioned behavior patterns from what the human and the Universal Natures intended. Eating and drinking in accordance with these rather strict dietary laws places man's systems in balance, and further, leads him to the state allowing unification, creative contemplation, and the realm of high spirituality.

From the Gospel of Luke (21:34), Jesus states very plainly: "See that you do not make your minds heavy, by never eating meat or drinking wine." This from the Aramaic text of the Evangelion DaMepharreshe, the oldest text of the Gospels know to exist.

Spoken to Adam and Eve in the Garden of Eden (Genesis 1:29) "Behold, I have given you every herb bearing seed, which is upon the face of all the earth, and every tree, in which is the fruit of a tree yielding seed; to you it shall be for meat."

Removing disease from one's body cleanses the vessel that will house the created purified energy and is, therefore, of extreme importance to students of Pure Mind practice.

The basics, though not yet fully perfected, can be found in the ever-evolving techniques of macrobiotics. Here we find "healing" that comes from natural law which governs all creatures, plants, etc. It is here that we find the balance enabling man to choose his destiny.

Macrobiotics, based on the Eastern philosophy of Yin-Yang, has been taught throughout the centuries by the great Eastern spiritual leaders. This way of being has been greatly overshadowed by Western "cure" methods and economics. It is not only an individual's physical and/or mental ailments that need to be addressed, as they are by Western medicine, but society's as well. ***Man's diseases which include unhappiness, stress, violence, crime, etc. all result, in part, from his behavior which violates human and Universal Natures.***

It would be too naive a premise to accept that man could cure all his problems with a macrobiotic diet and philosophy, but macrobiotics in its purest formulation can take a person a long way in allowing him to unite in harmony with nature by stopping his violations of its laws. The true medicines of the mind are high spiritual awakenings and manifestation of Universal Nature's design of man's purpose. A disease free body and mind, the Pure Mind Path, and a deep inner faith are the tools for these high or deep spiritual awakenings.

There have been many books, articles, and papers written on the subject of macrobiotics, and the research goes on. But be aware, like the religions of today, macrobiotics are watered down, contaminated versions of very old principles, and should be viewed as a thread of truth propelled by economic and self-serving corruption. This text is not the place to carry this discourse further. Our job is to make you aware of the great problems that an out of balance body/mind creates. It is your duty to yourself and your practice to research and correct these problems. Of course the master teacher is your own body and the acute awareness gained through Pure Mind practice is the premier student.

Having touched on diseases created by the ingestion of toxic foods and air, let us move to the mind which gathers impurities from our physical body's diseased condition, our imagined fears, our acceptance of perverted truth, as well as our environment. The human mind creates stress, frustration, emotional disappointments through many forms of wrong understanding, especially in our adaptation of diluted partial-truth belief systems both in the social and spiritual realms. If we are to have spiritual development we must eliminate all these layers of impurities.

The Pure Mind Path, which is the mirror reflection of Universal Nature itself, has been split into many disciplines dating as far back as its beginning on Earth almost one hundred thousand years ago. One example of this splintering is the five thousand year old Yogic science which itself was split into two branches, the healing and the spiritual, and now has been split even further beyond its physical and mental practices and study. Even so, separate or together, any successful effort by a student of any discipline largely depends upon a body/mind that is free from all disease.

These separations unfortunately were created by man's insatiable leaning towards laziness along with his need to create something new for his own ego and/or economic goals. As always he is left with a path that is, for the most part, useless. Even the advanced Yogic science students of today find themselves practicing in many different combinations in order to grasp the whole ideal, but are failing to do so by leaving out two very important disciplines: Tantra and the Pure Mind awakenings of Universal Nature's purpose. If we were to put all these splinter disciplines back together we would have Yoga, Vedanta, and Yaur-veda as one practice

chapter 7   *Our Living Practice*   *18*

(Buddhism broke away twenty-five hundred years later). Practiced as one discipline we would have true methods of meditation, health, and healing methodologies for both the physical and mental, all working together. If we add Tantra we add the means to change the nature of our consciousness. If we sprinkle in the threads of truth hidden in other Eastern and Western religions and we blanket them all with the true purpose of human life, we would have circled back to the original discipline: the Pure Mind Path.

The diseases that stem almost entirely from physical causes can and should be treated on a physical level. Psychologically generated diseases create the long lasting imbalances and problems. In most cases the physical and psychological cannot be separated. No matter which is diseased, there's an imbalance consequence on the other.

~:*All Yogic and Buddhist practices stem from Pure Mind awakenings and methods. Though greatly diluted they nevertheless contain many seeds of Truth and methodology inherited from their mother discipline. THE ONE OVERPOWERING AND GRAVELY SOLEMN TRUTH THAT HAS BEEN TOTALLY DISTORTED, VILIFIED OR FORGOTTEN IS THAT "THE FULFILLMENT OF OUR TRUE NATURE IS A MATTER OF BECOMING, NOT JUST A MAT-*

TER OF BEING." THAT IS ULTIMATE WIS-DOM BEYOND WISDOM.

Think! Do not allow yourself to be educated and conditioned to be exploited by the system. If you do not break your chains, you will never know the freedom, love, and joys that animals, plants, and high spiritual achievers know.

Our movement toward the awakening of Universal Truth is greatly dictated by the condition of the vehicle in which we travel, how we use that vehicle, and the tracks we travel on. The foods we eat, the air we breathe, the liquids we drink, the chemicals we ingest, the thoughts we think, and the emotions we feel form our vehicle. Each time we eat a nutritionless, processed, or chemically laden food, sip polluted water, inhale polluted air, cause abuse and killing of a sentient being by eating its flesh, we taint our bodies and minds with disease and in turn we taint our energy. Tainted energy will not attract the transference of an energy essence vessel nor can one be created by a diseased and/or unbalanced mind/body. Unless we make every effort to rid ourselves of unnatural substances, we will fail in our life purpose as humans.

Meditation, chanting, work, relationships, dancing, walking, exercising, etc. are the uses of our vehicle. Meditative practice, the books we read, the teacher, chapter 7   *Our Living Practice*

and our destination are the tracks we travel on. It is wrong to think that these separate parts make up the whole of one's being. The important principle of binding, or polarization, is missing. Whether in the phenomena world, spiritual dimensions, or in the eternal vessel we create, all is bound by Universal Nature via its Breath of Life. The old quote, "There is nothing new under the sun" can be seen as coming from the realization that all things reflect all things. The eternal principle of being In-Perpetuum reflects Universal Nature, as an In-Perpetuum Being's eternal energy vessel reflects Universal Nature's infinity.

It would be ponderous and unnecessary for me to detail all correct living practice according to Pure Mind understanding, except to say that if one follows both human and Universal natural law so that his relationship is in harmony with those laws, he can be assured that he is correct in his actions.

Working, dancing, chanting, sitting, sex, exercising, etc. should all flow with natural rhythm. Universal Nature's rhythm is seen as fairly constant by those who are awake and aware. The phenomena world, being made up of many natures, has many rhythms. These are easily felt by those in touch and in harmony with them. Humans have their own natural rhythm and ways of being which are unfortunately misinterpreted by dogmatic, scientific, and/or self-serving thinkers. Through Pure Mind practice we awaken to what is natural in all natures. We learn almost immediately that parts do not make up the whole, and so we recognize not to stress any or all individual parts, desires, needs, or practices as other than complementary. *We attempt to live our whole life as a reflection of Universal Nature which binds all natures, and that is our practice.*

~Traceless

A wayfarer I am; flowing
like a never ending stream,
living the life of a cloud
ever drifting to somewhere,
pausing a moment, then
moving on to nowhere.

Traceless I am, akin to
the blowing wind.
If you search carefully you
will see my shadow caressing
sunlit mountain peaks, and feel
me dancing with your hair.~

Chapter Eight
Love, Kindness, Compassion, and Sensitivity

The Heart and Soul of Pure Mind Practice

*"If Truth is indeed in and around everything
how is it that I cannot see it?"*
Simply because you're in the way.

~tears which you
give no voice to
speak of love~

chapter 8   The Heart & Soul   1

I will guide my thoughts and actions to be filled with love, compassion and kindness for all living things.

These are the words that conclude our meditation sessions. As the Buddhists see their prayer flags, we put our words on the currents of the wind so that they will carry them throughout all worlds to help end suffering and bring about security and happiness to all living beings who are born or about to be born.

~:Love! First of all we must understand that what most people call love is in fact a mind state that is contrary to any hope of lasting happiness. This "love" is their mind's delusionary state which they settle for in their futile search for fullness.~:~ Since we have always been trained to use our minds to solve problems, to create or gather whatever we need from sources outside ourselves, we naturally look for that which is beyond; beyond our belief systems, beyond our reason, etc. Because we have turned to books, teachers, and prophets in the search for fullness, or "love," we have unwittingly turned our attention outward, and so depend on others to define who we are.

We choose marriage or life partners who are willing to give us what we seek and who further inflate our egos by providing approval and acceptance.

These people we label "compatible," and there are millions upon millions of "loving couples" born out of these false impressions which are pathological in nature. ~:This mental or physical "love" is illusory, because it drains energy and brings nothing more than short-term physical or ego satisfactions and leaves us in a long-term state of frustration and boredom.

Not knowing nor finding anything more fulfilling, humans try unsuccessfully to substitute this illusionary love for something most people unknowingly but deeply long for: eternal life with its joyful state of ecstasy. This longing or "hungry ghost" is a natural drive from Universal Nature to fulfill itself through all physical phenomena. *So there is no way of escaping this desire and no way to fulfill it from the outside.~:~*

~:We practitioners of the Universal Life Wheel do not, therefore, seek as love the illusions which are born out of the "mind," nor fulfillment of sexual drives and various emotions that stem from the same desirous nature. We seek and find true love which is born "inside" in a pure meditative state. This is love conceived with Universal Nature, carried and spread by the Universal Breath of Life. It is only this "love" that delivers fullness and eternal joy.~:~

~:Deep meditation brings an all-encompassing love that arises with a quality of understanding that spreads through and out of our body and mind. Here is where we find fullness, because we are totally consumed and thereby become love itself. When in a true meditative state everything starts to disappear—thought, physical pain, stress, everything—until there's nothing left except silence. It is not the rational understanding of a silent noiseless void, but instead the living silence that overflows with deep rich sound tones and a light that can only be seen by "seeing eyes" turned inward.~:~

~:This love found in meditation is not directed towards anybody; it is not a relationship but a quality of our being. We are not "in love," we are unconditional love, and loving unconditionally is eternal.~:~ It is what you would see and feel if you stood facing Jesus, Buddha, Moses, or Gandhi, as well as all other enlightened and reincarnated In-Perpetuum Beings.

Kindness: Simply put, it is the embodiment of the deep love we experience living the Universal Life Wheel with its Pure Mind meditation direction. It is the practice of kindness shown directly to all living things as proclaimed in the Right Living direction of the Wheel. ~:That is, treating each and every living thing in a kind and gentle manner. The principle is to cause no physical or mental harm or abuse, neither directly nor indirectly through our desires. ~:~The eating of flesh would be a prime example of fostering the abuse and killing of another sentient being.

~:An act of kindness, without an ulterior motive, is a pure way of giving up our idea of separateness and living our awakenings of "oneness." "All of the single root." In acts of kindness we proclaim no distinction between man and woman, teacher and student, earth and sky, that everything has the same value, everything is just as it is.~:~

All spiritual teachings and awakenings will be in vain when we do not manifest the love we garner into kindness and compassion. Contrary to some popular religious separatist beliefs, even the most exalted states and spiritual accomplishments become useless unless one lives his life with kindness. Knowing that love, kindness, and compassion play a major part in creating the binding energies for our vessel proves beyond a doubt that living in kindness is extremely valuable.

Compassion: A dictionary definition is "feeling and showing sorrow for others." But for those who awaken with love it is more, so very much more. ~:Compassion cannot be described in terms of "feeling or showing" for these things are for the most part short-lived and superficial. Compassion is something which is inherent in the human. It is not merely an applied something as a result of its creation. Through our Pure Mind Path we awaken and become the actualization of compassion. We learn to know the pain of suffering by others, but more importantly we learn to understand its roots, and finally how to bring suffering to an end. All these combined lead us to know that with our awakening and the love it brings, all living things will benefit. Understand that this is not our goal for it is not a goal of Universal Nature, but instead, a natural result of our successful efforts. When compassion is awakened, compassion will be manifested.

What you own and what you think
is how you will be remembered.
But is that what you are?

~:Compassion is one of a student's strongest awakenings. It will gently touch and caress you. This releases a feeling of ecstasy which fills you with joy, and the energy created explodes and pulsates and can be felt by others. Some call it your vibrations, and by those you'll be fondly remembered.~:~

Sensitivity: Living the Pure Mind Wheel you learn that the world and everything in it does not belong to you. It is not yours to use and abuse for your comfort and pleasure. Instead, we learn that we belong to everything in this world, in the universe. We are a small part of it; we are not the heart of it. It does not, nor should it be made to revolve around us. When you awaken to these truths you become sensitive to even the smallest of bugs, and they become important to you. You understand that even an amoeba is as important as the sun for without its existence we would be less. This amoeba is not replaceable; it has its own value, its own evolution.

Sensitivity creates a closeness with nature, with its animals, its flowers, its forests, its mountains, lakes and rivers. It brings you so much closer to stars, moons, and other universes with their living beings. As sensitivity grows so grows love, and as love grows your energy vehicle becomes more and more solidified, and you get closer to eternal being.

To live and love fully requires us to recognize and accept that we cannot possess nor own anything. This applies to material things as well as other people and includes our own bodies. ~:Knowing that spiritual joy, freedom, and wisdom do not come as a result of possession but rather through our capacity to open ourselves enables us to love more fully. The longing for and the movement towards love are another form of the "hungry spiritual ghost" that resides in all of humanity and is behind most of our activities.~:~

Most happiness that we experience in our lives is never about possessions or understanding but about our ability to love, to be free, and to have a wise relationship with our own lives. This awakening arises out of a sense of connection with all things.

Living a spiritual life may seem to most complicated, but in actuality it is the opposite. We find that simplicity leads to clarity even in the midst of this complex world. We are able to discover these things when we realize that it's the quality of the love, compassion, and kindness that we bring to our lives that matters the most.

~violet petals
pop open
misting my nose~

~:Without the Pure Mind Path body of knowledge, understanding, with its essence of love, kindness, and compassion, meditation exercises that point you to awakening are a waste of effort.~:~

Awakening is not the focus of our Pure Mind practice. To guide practitioners to open themselves like the petals of a rose is its object and therefore our focal point.

Chapter Nine
Mindfulness

"truth lies in the grass
and in the soil
those who see
take off their shoes"
Through Zen to E. B. Browning

Try and be a sheet of paper with nothing on it.
Be a spot of ground where nothing is growing,
where something might be planted,
a seed, possibly, from the Absolute.
Rumi

~reeling amongst
flowers, drunk with
moon fumes~

~coyote's frozen shadow
mooning cottontail
caught napping~

In this moment in time is captured the essences of being mindful and unmindful by two creatures in the same moment.

~:Mindfulness in everyday life and in meditation is in itself a practice of the highest priority. Without it there can be no meditative state nor would a meaningful life be possible. Mindfulness is a state of being in this very moment, at this very moment.~:~

~:Live solely in *each* present moment with an attitude of a spectator, that is, the "self" that sees with pure observation, and it is through this attitude that clear knowledge can be obtained. The practice of mindfulness brings one's mind under control and to a state of rest helping to bring insight into the threefold itness of I, us, universality* and thus to a clearer insight of the Universal Nature of all existence. Seen in this way mindfulness can be a basis for deep awakening.~:~

Throughout Pure Mind meditation practice we create a state of **clear awareness,** or mindfulness, and give to each and every experience our full attention. This is how we recognize when any part of

---
*seeing everything as it is, as a separate form with its own nature and at the same time as one with its immediate surrounding and further with the universe.

lives and/or meditation practice is deteriorating so we may correct it at that very moment.

The Universal Life Wheel must be lived with a mindful attitude, because this makes you aware of your activities in every moment. It is through Pure Mind practice that you will find the meaning of life as a sentient being, and then you will have the meaning of your everyday activity. ~:Living this way we are not special; we are, in fact, just living in the manner we should.~:~

Right mindfulness is the blood that flows through us and the core of our practice. Being mindful is the key for knowing the mind and thus is our starting point. It is the perfect tool for shaping our minds and thus the focal point of our practice.

~:Since the state of In-Perpetuum is the lofty manifestation of our practice, and that practice depends greatly upon right mindfulness, becoming an In-Perpetuum Being can also be said to be the culminating point.~:~

Even though mindfulness is so highly praised throughout various spiritual traditions for its capacity to generate great achievements, it is not at all a secret mystical state, and is within the reach of all people. It is something quite simple, common, and familiar to us. In this simplest manifestation, we know it as "attention."

Mindfulness is also the prime function of consciousness; without it we have no perception of any object at all. When an object stimulates the senses, attention is aroused in its basic form and an initial "first notice" takes place. This happens thousands of times during every second of our waking lives. This initial attention is of decisive importance for it is the first "touching" of the subconscious by the conscious.

In this first perception phase only a very general and indistinct picture of the object results. If there is any further interest in the object or if its impact on our senses is very strong, our attention will be focused on the details. Now our attention will be directed toward its characteristics, also on its direct relationship to us. Here is where our mind compares its present perception with similar ones recollected from our past. This is exactly how we coordinate our experiences. This stage is an important step in mental development and shows the close and constant connection between memory and mindfulness, or attention. Without memory, attention towards an object would give us merely isolated facts, as in the case of most of the perceptions of animals. This is important and should be understood. *It is from this associative thinking that the next important step in evolutionary devel-*

opment is derived. Here we must include the capacity of abstract thinking in this second stage of cognition being affected by the development of mindfulness. So we can see four characteristics of this second stage: 1) an increase in detail; 2) reference to the observer, or subjectivity; 3) connective or associative thinking; and 4) abstract thinking.

By far the greatest part of understanding for the human takes place on the plane of the second phase. This second phase covers a wide field ranging from any attentive observation of everyday facts through an attentive occupation with any work from research being done by scientists to the subtle thoughts of the philosopher. ~:Here perception is certainly more detailed and comprehensive, but *it is not necessarily more reliable. Perception is more or less adulterated by contaminated memory association and emotions, intellectual prejudices, wishful thinking, etc., and primarily by the delusion of either a conscientious or an unconscious assumption of a permanent substance inherent in things or of a soul in living things.* ~:~Because of any or all of these factors, the reliability of even the most common perceptions and judgments may be seriously impaired. Without guidance an overwhelming percentage of people remain stuck in this second stage of perception; these include those who do not apply this knowledge to the systematic training of their minds.

chapter 9   *Mindfulness*   5

~:Gradually advancing in the development of attentiveness, we enter the domain of right mindfulness. We call it "right" because it keeps the mind free from false influences, because it is the basis of right understanding, because it teaches us to do the right things in the right way.~:~

The objects of perception and thought, having gone through the sifting process of keen analysis as prepared by right mindfulness, are therefore reliable material for all other advanced mental functions (theory evaluation and judgment, ethical decisions, etc.), and most notably these now undistorted actualities form a solid basis for Pure Mind meditation; for example, viewing all phenomena as impermanent and void of substance. Undistorted actualities also form the basis of the Pure Mind Universal Life Wheel everyday living practice. To be sure, the high level of clarity offered by right mindfulness will, to an unprepared mind, be anything but familiar. At best an untrained mind may occasionally touch the edge of undistorted clarity, but in treading the way dictated by this Universal Wheel, right mindfulness can grow into something very familiar. Right mindfulness performs the same functions as the two lowest stages of development, though it does so on a much higher plane. ~:The functions common to right mindfulness are producing an increasingly greater clarity and intensity of consciousness, presenting an image of actuality that increasingly filters out any falsifications.~:~

With this brief outline of the evolution of mental processes as mirrored by the actual stages and quality differences of perception, we can see the faint awareness of the object becoming a more distinct perception, and gain a more detailed knowledge of it. Traveling from perception of isolated facts to the discovery of their causal mental connections, we go from a still defective, inaccurate, or prejudiced cognition to the clear and undistorted presentation by right mindfulness. We have also seen how it is an increase in intensity and quality of attentive mindfulness that is mainly instrumental in the transition to the next higher dimension.

> ~kneeling alongside
> the crop row
> listening to a worm~

The mind functions to attach objects to memory. In doing so it expands. What is mind if not an accumulation of past memories of thoughts, objects, and experiences? As we gather these things our minds expand. One of the great awakenings has shown that every day more and more junk is collected. Your "mind" grows bigger and bigger ***but you have less and less consciousness.*** We are constantly repeating thoughts, and these thoughts are a repetition of our accumulated past. ~:***Thinking is*** *never original, because you can only think in terms of the known. Nothing new comes through. You cannot think about the unknown, you can only reach the unknown when you are not thinking.~:~*

Let the past rest in the past; think only this moment. The irony of this is that if you are **really in this moment, you cannot think; it is not possible.**

Thinking is only focused on the past or about the future, never in the present moment. **~:Remain in the moment. Live moment to moment, forget your past as well as the future, so that whatever you're doing becomes meditative.~:~** For example, when you look at a weed and really see it, the weed is no longer just a weed and you are no longer just you. The weed and you dissolve into something beyond what can be explained logically, but we **experience it.** This is clear seeing without thought, and we may understand the pure elation of as-it-is-ness, suchness, or itness.

So, we have two different usages of the word mindfulness. In its simplest form we see it as "being there," that is, being in the very moment, and we have the more complex usage, as in right perception of reality; but both definitions are co-dependent and therefore each cannot exist without the other.

Example of "being there":

~just sitting my
mind emptied,
so I threw it away~

Example of a right perception of reality:

~without me
he wouldn't exist
no temple gardens~

Chapter Ten

Pure Mind Understanding

Reincarnation, Creation,
Life as an In-Perpetuum Being,
The Breath of Universal Life,
Suffering, Awakening Energy,
The Final Life Moment

Ultimate truth
transcends logical
thought..........

Analytical, logical, linear, systematic, and scientific thought processes employed by scholars, scientists, intellectuals, and the like are a totally useless means of reaching and understanding Truths that lie beyond the physical dimensions. People using these methods of thinking when attempting to understand spiritual dimensions and realities therein always come up empty and frustrated. And yet they will dismiss, out of hand, what their minds cannot grasp. What you're about to read is not a metaphor, nor an analogy, nor is it based on intuition, nor simply one possibility among many. It is Universal Truth, and it should be taken literally. Until the "mind types" reach beyond their mind's physical limitations to spiritual realities, they will probably view this as fantasy. So be it!

~:Reincarnation:
It is the process increasing one's existence infinitely. There is only one Way to achieve the state of eternal being with perpetual life cycles and that is with Pure Mind awakening and embodiment. Those who see promises or a threat in that statement are unsuitable for Pure Mind practice. There are no threats or promises implied with this Truth, only in man's interpretation of it.

Attracting the teachings and transference of an energy vessel with the karmic effect of an In-Perpetuum Being requires many things from an individual: a deep practice, the creation and sustaining of purifying energies from his body/mind, awakening at all levels, and the embodiment of those awakenings. The pure energies he creates attach to the transferred vessel enabling those energies to dissolve continually back into themselves. The binding energies which hold the vessel together are created by the heart, one filled with love, compassion, and kindness.~:~

~:The sum total of all the student's purified energies including enlightened thoughts, correct attitudes, personality traits, etc., dissolve into the initial donated purified vessel of energy. This newly expanded vessel dissolves into itself and that self dissolves into itself. This process continues on until the student transcends to the point where he is wholly an energy vessel. This vessel spontaneously evolves to the state of a perpetual energy being that is totally liberated from mind and body forms.~:~

~:Having reached the state of an In-Perpetuum Being, he remains in the formless state of timelessness and spacelessness until such time as he returns as a sentient human form. This first reincarnation is without personal choice of form, time, or galaxy, unless the form was defined by a reincarnate (teacher or other) when the student was still in the physical form of his awakening. From then on, while in the physical state of reincarnation, he can choose his own destiny, either as a sentient or not. But if he chooses not, he may choose a still further reincarnation to return as a sentient. His third choice is just to return as part of an evolution without defining it, as was the case for his original reincarnation.~:~

Through practice Pure Mind Path students of awakening learn to recognize that all the virtuous aspects which made up their personalities and permeated their actions by living the Universal Life Wheel persist after shedding body/mind. This is due to the pure energy field vessel and the binding energies they created. They also fully understand that all things are impermanent, because as they go from chosen form to chosen form and from aeon to aeon, their energy vessel changes. Just as some adherents to this practice gradually evolve from sentient beings to Beings In-Perpetuum, so will they evolve from that perpetual being to their new life form, bringing with them their relatively long-term characteristics which help determine their "now" personalities.

This knowledge that character and personality persist in reincarnation (impermanency is a matter of form, partial form, degree, and time) makes it easy to understand the recognition of heredity factors seen in reincarnates.

~Freeing the mind/body
my mortality
became immortal~

Creation:
"In the beginning, God created heaven and earth." This, of course, is the start of the Old Testament. Let me ask you, was this God a spirit, a person, a thing? Was it male, female, or both? Did it have a consciousness and why did he, she, or it, create? The Bible's proclamation of God's creation and all the questions that statement raises can lead your mind far away into an imaginary beyond, and when you imagine an omnipotent "God" as a premise, all the conclusions that you arrive at will only be your imagination at work.

~:What if the creator of which the Bible speaks was actually "thought?" Such thought that leads straight back to mind and heart. You may begin to recognize how, instead of leading you to an imaginary beyond, the recognition of thought as the basis for creation leads to a solid starting point: the mind. This mind becomes the focal point, and when it is liberated and purified, the mind becomes the culminating point.~:~

Through mind alone are we aware of the external world including our bodies, so it follows that if we can understand this "mind," we will have placed ourselves in a position to understand all things. In order to do this we must turn inward to find a path leading beyond the boundaries of our own ego minds. This can be a very slow process, but if the methods are practiced correctly, with loving kindness and compassion, *the answers never fail to arrive.* ~:We find that there is a strong and well ordered inner center deep in our minds, where all our confusion can dissolve and energy forces can spontaneously gather around the Breath of Universal Life, revealing to us its knowledge in a clear way.~:~

~:We must recognize that this center of our mind, which is so much a part of us, is unknown to us; that the conscious mind which we see as unwieldy and obstinate can, with great effort, be made pliant; that the "freeing" of the mind is something we can accomplish here and now. In view of this, we might have started this chapter with, "In the beginning there is Universal Nature, therein resides its realm of all latent possibilities, and wherein resides Universal Nature's single, powerful, and perpetual thought: to know itself. To know its nature, the Self Nature beyond self, including the nature, manifestation, and final evolution stage of all mental and physical possibilities." Because of this pure powerful thought, a single latent possibility is energized by the one remaining In-Perpetuum energy vessel whose sole objective is to do just that: energize the one possibility which starts the cycle all over again.

Through countless light-years of Universal Nature's need "to know," In-Perpetuum Beings energize most of the remaining latent possibilities. When all those phenomena evolve nearing their natural end, all sentient beings will have reached the highest state of consciousness. They, in turn, direct their thoughts to a single thought of knowing, the knowing of that which is yet to be known. At that same time all remaining latent phenomena are energized and manifested, and they come to be fully known. Beyond this point all evolutionary life processes come to their natural end. With this "end" there is a "beginning" for, as always, all that remains is: Universal Nature with its one powerful thought to know itself, and therein lies its realm of latent possibilities, and therein resides a single In-Perpetuum Being with its one powerful objective..........~:~

We shall not cease from exploration,
And at the end of all our exploring
We will arrive where we started
And know the place for the
very first time.
      T.S. Elliot

~:Man's means of exploration beyond the physical realms is the Pure Mind Path with its Univer-

sal Life Wheel, because its practice places mind/body in right motion.~:~As we have learned, this direction polarizes and expands the energy vessel which, when liberated from the physical, remains as an In-Perpetuum Being. As we have also come to learn, this Being's ultimate "purpose" is to be an energizer of all phenomena possibilities.

"It is best not to seek that which is seemingly far away, beyond the realm of experience and therefore beyond our comprehension when you cannot even see what is very close to you."

unknown

~:Origin is no less or more than a combining of energy with a latent possibility having its own nature. It is from these origins that all phenomena flow. Phenomena differ from cycle to cycle, because each time a possibility is energized to life, it bears the "personality signature" of the energy essence consciousness from which it sprang, and yet it is always the same, for all phenomena spring from Universal Nature.~:~

~:Student practitioners of the Universal Life Wheel will come to unravel life's mysteries as they travel beyond their limited minds to a union with Nature and become acquainted with their own origin. They are travelers who pass on in haste and separate from self as smoke separates from fire. Their travels are a succession of truths awakened, leading them away from darkness and dualistic thinking.

They travel onward, higher and higher, transfiguring their vessel with more and more energy and binding it more solidly with love and compassion, until they separate from mind/body to become or remain as In-Perpetuum Beings.~:~

~:The illusionary world of what lies beyond in the spiritual realm, as with the basis of most religions, rests on incorrect interpretations of partial realities.~:~ A person's illusions are very real to him, and they create a great deal of tainted energy, an energy usually enhanced by false joy and momentary happiness. In the near future the loss of this same joy and happiness will bring him a great amount of suffering, emptiness and disillusionment.

~:In a tainted spiritual search, imagination leads a person to the point, as in formal religions, where one's practice becomes only a belief system and only blind acceptance remains as an answer. You may come to a point where the practice takes you as far as it is able, as with Zen Buddhism, a practice that may take you beyond the human condition of suffering as was described by the historical Buddha, and is, as I see it, the basis for modern psychology. However, if the Zen boat or any other vehicle has taken you to its limits, it's time to bow out and find "the" boat that will carry you to the point of total awakening and immortality. The Pure Mind Path does exactly that by progressing beyond the point where all others stop; beyond faith, to the experience of the deepest awakenings.~:~

>~Having climbed
>religion's mountain,
>it's time to begin.~

>~Awake at last
>I flow into
>the spring night.~

~:When first energized by an In-Perpetuum Being, a species has the purity of that which has not yet been contaminated by human mind. Contamination begins as a species materializes into form, the start of its evolution. The moment before materialization is when unenlightened beings see this event as a "miracle," as a God-like revelation, because knowledge of its true origin is beyond man's level of human consciousness.~:~

~:Ultimately all origination is no more or less than a combining of energy with a latent possibility having its own nature. It is from this event that all phenomena flow. Energizing can only take place after

chapter 10   Pure Mind Understanding   10

In-Perpetuum Beings pass out of physical form. Yet all definitions of possibility take place while they're in physical human form.~:~

The following is transcribed from a tape placed by my pillow to record my utterances which, at that time, were occurring frequently while I was in a meditative state. I believe that the following, which was recorded about two weeks after my first deep awakening, is a continuation of an earlier enlightenment I had awakening me to the process of defining and energizing latent possibilities by In-Perpetuum Beings.

M. Agass

Possibilities, billions of possibilities, latent, waiting, not waiting; no voice,
no expectations, no breath, no life, no death.
When is its time? long pause..........

Being is time. But when? Does being have a time when it is its time...is that when time becomes energized to form? Ever waiting for neither exists separately...so what's waiting, time or being? pause.....

With no breath, no life, no voice, no thoughts, no feeling, what then is waiting? Perhaps its creation will be as an "it", can it later be a form of another time/space?...for now, it has being in time, what if it wasn't its time for being...is its time still latent? Is it still possible as a new creation? long pause.....

Waiting, not waiting, stillness, no time flowing. Will it be energized to form? Waiting, not waiting, ever in the rich silent sounds of non-being.
Ending gong sounded.

Some might say that this is just my conscious mind rambling on with thoughts that were sparked by my previous awakening. But I know that these sounds came to my conscious mind from a spiritual dimension I had entered through a meditative state.

Suffering:
The Historical Buddha and Being In-Perpetuum, Siddhartha Gautama, after a much disputed length of time spent in a meditative state, reawakened and after having taken a little time to enjoy the supreme bliss resulting from his renewed spiritual liberation, preached his first sermon in Deer Park on the subjects of the Four Noble Truths. He also spoke of the Middle Way which he found lay between the extremes of sensual indulgence and self-mortifications. He was about thirty-five when he reawakened and lived to about eighty. So Buddhism did not begin with the answers to great metaphysical questions like, "What is the meaning of life?", "What happens when we die?", and proving the existence of God. Rather, its root principle is that all human existence is imperfect in a very deep way. Therefore, "Suffering I teach, and the way out of suffering," the Buddha declared and began teaching the doctrine of the Four Noble Truths:

First Truth: Suffering exists.
Second Truth: Suffering has an identifiable cause.
Third Truth: The causes of suffering can be termi-

nated.
Fourth Truth: is the means of its elimination.

These Four Noble Truths have been interpreted, commented on, and reinterpreted, all this being housed in great bodies of work and commentaries on those works. Unfortunately, like the words of Jesus Christ and many others, most of the essence and therefore the true meaning of what was and is being transmitted was misinterpreted.

Let us look at the Buddha's words in their true light. We start with: all humanity's existence is characterized by suffering which cannot bring satisfaction in any healthy form. Due to their level of understanding and life practice, people experience suffering in everything they do: birth, sickness, death, having the experiences they do not like, being separated from that which they do like, and not obtaining what they desire. Then we should add the principle traits of attachment: form, sensations, perception, mental formations and consciousness. Since craving and desire attach themselves to those traits, it makes them objects of attachments which cause suffering and all its illusions. Further still, sensual craving and ego desires bind humans to illusion.

Up to this point all understandings are pretty standard and correct, but here truth and the standard interpretations are widely separated. The true meaning and essence of the "Awakened One's" words for the Third and Fourth Noble Truths state: all sentient human beings exist for the purpose of liberating their body and minds from suffering and in the process will aid in liberating all sentient beings from suffering and further invoke the true karmic law of eternal being.

~:This cause and effect, or karma, is best understood by its opposite face of non-cause/non-effect leading to dispersion of form and energy, which is what all unaware sentient beings are faced with when passing on (death).~:~ Simply stated, non-recognition of the Pure Mind Path as the only true, direct means for creating the necessary results to attract an In-Perpetuum teacher, and/or a person recognizing Universal Truth but failing to adopt the life practice of the Universal Wheel, sets in motion the natural law (at this point in time) of no cause, thereby no effect, which results in the dispersion of human form and consciousness.

~:Liberation and freedom create the karmic energy body of an In-Perpetuum Being, as opposed to that which is widely believed.~:~

~press on
dung beetle
it's a long winding hill~

Most of suffering and pain comes from frustrations which create a great deal of mental stress. The human thinking process, which is strictly dualistic at this point in its evolution, asks or seeks something in return for its efforts, time, and/or affection. This naturally leads to expectations, and those expectations can be called the root cause of frustration and suffering. Possibly the most glaring example comes from the human's expectations of being "in love." People expect many things both from the person they love and from the act itself. Such expectations and anticipations are the basis of unfulfilled promises, disappointment, stress, and inevitably some degree of hate. An expectation of love to be returned places the other person in a state of bondage, making love a duty to be discharged, something that must be done. This type of love relationship is never fulfilling, because it is not freely given. Bondage is a tremendous burden for one to carry, especially when the cause of it is another person demanding, even begging for love. At this point there is only resentment. ~:Love originating in emotion or sensory desire dies very quickly, for anything that seemed beautiful about it is lost in unfulfilled expectations. **When you love with expectation, you kill it, it is dead, period.** Love cannot exist if there is something you want out of it.~:~

~:Love is an end unto itself. Loving another is the

end. No expectations, no demands, no desires except to love.~:~

When love is not a give and take situation, you can never be frustrated for nothing is expected. On the other hand, people also hope love will end their frustrations of loneliness, sexual desires, etc. Here love as they seek it comes with strings, or again, expectations and, therefore, it is not a pure emotion but a striking of a bargain, a give and take "deal." If you ask nothing in return, you will not have expectations and, therefore, there will be no frustration forthcoming.

~:When your emotions are pure and freely given, your whole being fills with love; these energies with their pure ecstasy and joy are the very energies we seek and must create to maintain our eternal energy vessels.~:~

We can find many examples of this type of love in everyday life, that is, where you have the freedom to love openly and fully for you do not have any expectations of it being returned. Unfortunately, these loves are almost exclusively for things that are other than human. You cannot ask for or place a burden (though some try with sentient animals) of expectations upon them. So they have nothing of your expectations to live up to, and they are free to love as they choose.

~:The simple pure act of love is a total giving— asking nothing in return. Being unconditional love leaves one free to love anywhere, anytime, and anyone without fear of frustration, disappointment, and suffering.~:~

People in general are frustrated. They have ideals and great expectations. They live in a society and expect it to conform to their ideals of right and wrong. They formulate a utopian model of life which no one, including themselves, can live up to. They not only expect too much, they also expect immediate transformation by themselves as well as by the world. Unfortunately, the world does not take heed and goes on its merry way resulting in more frustration.

The cause or object of frustration makes no difference, but love, power, wealth, religion, and God are the greatest causes. Seeking wealth and/or power creates many expectations and illusions, for these things call for cooperation and bargains with others. Religion is a structure which should release frustration, yet is a greater cause of it. It proposes to bring you closer to God, so it offers something you seek in return for your devotion. ~:The search for God is probably the most devastating, because it is Universal Nature's desire for you to awaken that is the driving force behind that desire, and so it is very deep and natural.~:~ And therefore a search for "God" is really a search for Truth, but having an omnipotent being as the object of your search leads to a wholly misguided quest and more unanswered questions. ~:This God search carried on through meditation, prayer, or any formal religious structure begins with the expectation of finding or knowing, and here again you have the great playing field of suffering. Know that if you stop your seeking with expectations, and love openly and freely, asking nothing in return, Truth will come to you, fill you, and be with you for eternity.~:~

The Universal Life Wheel may be very difficult indeed, but the other paths are impossible. Once again we must mention the improbability of logical thinkers stepping beyond their minds' limitations in order to think of this reality as other than fantasy. If it had not been part of Mahan Agass' reawakening to experience anew the following occurrences, we would probably have come to the same conclusion. For a moment stop and consider that without programmed reincarnation resulting in eternal being, we still would have no answers. Nevertheless, by refusing to go beyond their conditioned logical thinking and cognitive "comfort zones" (no matter their present state of spiritual practice, if any), they disassociate themselves from any further spiritual possibility and any chance of experiencing all the deeper Truths.

"Those who dance are considered insane by those who cannot hear the music." George Carlin?

Reawakened In-Perpetuum Beings view with amusement the awe and wonderment shown by those who are in the process of reawakening. Such was the case when Mahan approached them about the authenticity of the following enlightened awakenings. These awakenings were first transmitted to him after his initial reawakening to being a Perpetual Being. Some of these phenomenal truths, he had come to learn, he experienced in other lifetimes, and were being reexperienced by him in this lifetime. Awe inspiring experiences leading to awakened truths are achievable in advanced student practitioners of the Pure Mind Path with the exception of those occurrences dependent on being in a formless state or having been in that state and are presently reincarnated.

The realization that a student's success greatly depended on his awakening to and accepting the following indisputable Universal Truth, because it is the primary premise of Pure Mind practice, and therefore, his practice, placed great pressure on Mahan's ability to communicate successfully the following enlightened truths.

Life As an In-Perpetuum Being:
~:This being/non-being flows in and out of life

form thousands of times during any one cycle (the number partially depends on when within a cycle he attains his eternal state). Whether in physical form or not, there is always life, always things happening. To believe that to be in physical form is the only instrumentality for living is ridiculous. All energy is alive. Although it may be dormant at times, it's still very much existent, it's just a matter of whether senses are affecting it or not. A lot of things happen in the break between two physical forms. Senses have no bearing on whether the In-Perpetuum Being is alive. Having a body form is one means of his existence, and that existence is primarily for experiencing the evolutionary progression of that period of time of whenever, wherever, and through whatever form he chooses to be reincarnated in. As earthling, it is only without the interference of body and mind that he finds the spiritual dimensions, so for anyone to believe there is no life beyond body, mind, and senses is to say, "There are no spiritual dimensions to be known or experienced." It would be a travesty to accept energy and spirituality as non-living dimensions. Awareness and consciousness are very much present when we are in a non-being formless form. It's an important part of Universal Nature's need to know itself.~:~

There is also some misconception about time. As long as something is in form, time will exist, although it doesn't exist for that which is not or yet to be in form, but since Eternal Beings always exist as an energy form or in some other form, time "keeps on ticking" as the cycle of Universal Life keeps on moving towards its end.

~:For a great number of reasons, such as energizing a latent possibility, or energizing another being's vessel after that being passes from physical form, energy vessels and their bindings dissipate, wear down, or are thinned. Therefore, one of the primary reasons In-Perpetuum Beings reincarnate to a human form is to rejuvenate and rebuild their pure energy vessel. Actually a lot of energy is lost and tarnished while an In-Perpetuum Being is in human sentient form, especially because humans are infantile in their evolution. Until the Perpetual Being begins his turn inward toward spirituality and his reawakening, his energy continues to dissipate.~:~ To answer the obvious question at this point, yes, an In-Perpetuum Being can lose that precious eternal state. It has happened, but not often.

~:Movement while out of form is by attraction of energies. In-Perpetuum Beings are not bound by either time or space and are in constant motion throughout the galaxies. They are attracted to various stars, planets, or solar systems by energy forces. That's how they're able to "visit" other species and planets inhabited by sentient or non-sentient life forms. Briefly experiencing life on any planet, while out of a sensory bodily form, is simply a matter of choosing a being who is in the process of creating a great deal of energy (usually of a sexual nature or of similar activity) and entering that being's body along with the new energies that he is creating. The In-Perpetuum Being's awareness is affected by the "host" body's pure senses, but not his mental interpretations.~:~ This practice, I'm sure, sounds like fun, and can be, but it is also very serious when it comes to choosing future incarnations. Leaving the host usually takes place while he sleeps. He, for the most part, is not aware of any of this, with the possible exception of a very long and intense "high" from the experience he was enjoying at the time the energy vessel entered.

~:After receiving an energy vessel and then passing out of physical form, if a student does not have a reincarnation defined by his teacher/guide, then the student must come back whenever and wherever a human type creature is born. Usually this takes place in about one hundred of earth's years, but to us it's measured as less than a blink of an earthling's eye. After that he can choose (or not) all his future reincarnations in that cycle. If he chooses to return in a form such as a flower or bird, he must also choose another reincarnation to follow that one, because he can only define when he is in a form that can think abstractly. If he chooses not to define the reincarnation that will follow after having lived the natural life as an eagle, for example, he'll return sometime as an abstract thinker in some form or another.~:~

~:An In-Perpetuum Being whose energy vessel is very powerful and plentiful due to his creation and incorporation of pure energies over many aeons of reincarnation places dormant energy "packets" into scores of worthy (defined as: depth of practice and attainment) students' bodies. The amount placed depends on the receiver's mental awareness, life practice, understanding, and potential to maintain the energies. After the receiver passes out of physical form, the donor energizes those dormant energies before they dissipate, and a new In-Perpetuum Being is "born." With this new Perpetual Being's old personality traits naturally cleansed and purified, together with the personality traits of the donor, the vessel is further polarized.~:~ This is a thumbnail sketch of a very complicated process but it is, nevertheless, how it transpires.

~:To be chosen for transference of an energy vessel by an In-Perpetuum Being enabling the most precious state of eternal being is exceptional. All seekers are first carefully screened as to their potential success in maintaining the state.~:~

~:The Breath of Universal Life:
It is the energy that contains, carries, and communicates the essence of Universal Nature. It is this essence of all Truth and wisdom that we awaken through deep meditative practice, and it is that energy (breath) that fills us with moments of ecstasy during the awakening process.~:~

To begin our study of the Breath of Life, we should not confuse our mystic physiological understandings of force flow through the human body with those of Western science. Ours is founded on subjective observations of our inner processes as opposed to "object isolating" investigations of science, i.e., self-observation and direct experience of processes and sensations within our own body, not on dissection of and/or external observation of animal organisms.

Western medical science is just beginning to recognize these energy force fields and their relation to human health, but medical scientists have a very long way to go to catch up with what is known in the East.

~:The Breath of Universal Life is not only subject to constant transformation, but is at the same time able to make use of various mediums of movement without interrupting its course. Think of an electric current and how it can flow through copper, iron, or water, and yet how it flashes through space without any medium when the tension is high enough, or how it moves in the form of radio waves. In this very same way the Breath of Life utilizes the blood, nerves, or the breath (inhalation) as conductors and, at the same time, moves and acts beyond and without these mediums into the infinity of space. This constant flow naturally moves through all form and space, but it is also at the command of In-Perpetuum Beings when, and if, they choose to concentrate it in order to direct its movement.

The Breath of Life is more than nerve-energy or the vital forces of the blood flow and much more than our breath. It is more than the creative powers of semen or the forces of nerves, more than the faculty of thought and intellect or willpower. All these are just modifications of the Breath of Universal Life.

To experience the Breath of Life within the human body, we must know and follow its movement through the five layers of human consciousness. The fifth layer, having the greatest density, is the physical body built up by nutrition. The fourth is the fine material layer sustained and nourished by breath and penetrates the physical body. The third is our thought body, our "personality," formed through active conscious thought. The second is the layer of our potential consciousness, which extends much deeper than our active thoughts (subconscious), and comprises the total of our spiritual capacities. The last and finest layer, which penetrates all previous ones, is the energy essence body (the Breath of Life) of the highest universal consciousness, which we practitioners nourish and sustain in ourselves with our powerful meditative energy and pure high energy emotions of love, kindness, compassion, and the exalted joy attained in a high conscious state. This layer is only experienced in a state of enlightenment or in the highest stages of meditative awakenings.

These layers are not separate in the human, but rather have the nature of mutually penetrating forms of energy, from the finest all-pervading, luminous Life Breath consciousness to the densest form of materialized consciousness which appears to us as physical bodies. All these layers work together. At the same time as the physical body is being built through nourishment, it is being penetrated and kept alive by the vital forces of inhalation and exhalation. In the same way, the active thought-consciousness penetrates the breath and helps determine the form the body will take. Thought, breath, and body are further penetrated and motivated by the still deeper consciousness of experience, intuition, and evolutionary information. Some call this our subconsciousness.

~:In the advanced states of meditation, when awakened, all this conscious and subconscious material, vital, and physical functions are further penetrated and transformed into spiritual energy through "inspiration and joy" until the essence of Universal Nature is revealed and becomes apparent. This is one of the foundations on which rests the Pure Mind Path and its meditative life practices.~:~

~:It is, therefore, only the spiritual mind/body created by the Pure Mind Path student which penetrates all five layers and thus integrates all his organs and faculties into one complete whole. *In this process of integration, of becoming whole and complete, awakened and enlightened, of creating purifying energies that dissolve back into themselves and flow into his new vessel, he further evolves to a liberated state of perpetual energy, and in this process lies the secret of immortality.~:~*

~:Those who do not attain this completeness and therefore identify with lesser values, with "parts of" or partial aspects, are subject to the laws of matter and all its components: *the law of mortality*. It would, therefore, be a mistake to ignore the value of our physical body, because even though our bodies are by nature limited, insofar as not being able to penetrate the other four layers, the body itself is penetrated by all other bodies. It thus becomes the natural stage of all spiritual decisions and movement and is the mediator between self and Self. The spiritualization of meditation, therefore, places the Breath of Life in its most accessible form for our awakening.~:~

~:Awakening Energy:
It is the only living link that connects us with the hidden forces of our pure natural "self." The concentrated calling up and direction of these forces is the concern and responsibility of reincarnated In-Perpetuum Beings. Of course, the teaching of enlightenment and its "dharma" paths is universal, but the evocation of new awakened knowledge and hence the evolutionary movement of the human species towards its final enlightened state is in the hands of reincarnates and their students who are striving to become as such.~:~

Having been asked many times to describe the awakening experience, we always repeat the words of Mahan Agass, "It is an instant happening in which we truly and completely forget ourselves when experiencing a higher reality. This can only be accomplished through an act of self-surrender which frees and transforms our innermost being. It's an ecstasy that fills us beyond our normal sensory capacities far greater than our prior experiences."

Energy is created by and for the human in many different ways, but for our purposes we need concern ourselves with only five. First, we create a certain amount of energy while we are in a state of rest. Second, we create a great deal of energy through both mental and physical exertion. The amount created is in direct proportion to the effort put out. Third, energy comes with an awakening experience, where the amount and power is directly related to the level or depth* of the awakening. Fourth is energy that we garner from outside. This can come from the rays of the sun, music that flows from natural rhythms, lightning, etc. Lastly, we can receive direct pure energy from an In-Perpetuum Being.

*There are five levels of awakening and the highest is the awakening to all Truth; this will usually happen in an immediate and direct manner.

~:All positive and pure energy is harnessed by its manifestation in living deeds and its embodiment into the character traits of the student, and bound together by the positive emotions of compassion, love, kindness, and Universal Truth's teachings of moral conduct.~:~

The energy that comes from awakening, due to its high level of power, is the energy used by "adepts" for things such as levitation, astral travel, and mind over matter demonstrations. But such uses of this energy are a waste of its purpose, and are considered a defilement by Perpetual Beings. It is, therefore, not practiced by reincarnates or their students. Unfortunately, we may see these energy vibration games performed by those whose practice is tainted and faulty and whose spiritual life practice is unfulfilled.

~:When the mind is abiding in silence, it's free from intellect and the human's ever-changing moralistic attachments. A being living in this pure free state sees unhampered by senses or dualistic thinking.~:~

The Final Life Moment:
~:Approximately 1200 years after Buddha's re-awakening and once again, as it had been every 12 to 15 years for hundreds of years prior, the word was being spread among the people that their precious Lama/Oracle would speak and teach the phowa. And so they came from lands far and near, most traveling by foot, some by small horse, and some by yak. Coming from Nepal, India, Burma, Kashmir, and the lowlands of China, they trekked on high through the Himalayan passes to Tibet. It took months for some as they passed through the treacherous conditions causing great physical and mental hardships. But for believers and practitioners of Buddhism, it was a blessing, not a hardship for they were coming to learn "how to die" so that they might never again have to live in this "hell" world of suffering.~:~

As people grow older they invariably face the important matter of life and death. Death, as the Tibetan tradition says, is a time when man must "face the moment when everything he has accumulated during his lifetime—loved ones, property, money, position and fame—must be left behind." Tibetan Buddhism comes the closest to the reality of knowing that the circumstances at the moment of our death can and will determine our future existence. They believe that by practicing the dictates in the Drikung Kagyu Phowa teachings, they would negate all their negative karma and open the crown exit door at the top of their heads. By further controlling the pathway of consciousness out of the body through the crown, and thereby into a higher realm, they avoid being reborn into the endless round of birth, death, and suffering. Their belief in controlling their energy's movement is not to allow it to leave the body through any of the other nine "doors of exit." Which of the other nine doors their consciousness flows out of dictates which realm of existence to which they will return. By practicing phowa at the moment of death, they believe their consciousness will be transferred directly to the Pure Land of the Buddha where they may attain enlightenment without the obstruction of body or mind. They also believe that any Buddhist practitioner with faith and confidence in Buddha's teachings may successfully practice phowa meditation.

As you can plainly see, this tradition and belief in the need for the practice of energy control and movement parallels closely the Pure Mind awakenings. ~:We now know that it is man's transcendent energy vessel that must depart the body through his third eye, not the crown. The practice traditions of the past will eventually be modified to reflect these newly awakened Truths. Modifications will include the understanding of Buddha's Four Noble Truths, impermanence, the law of cause and effect or karma, and the meaning for life as a human. It is only through the third eye exit that the bindings holding the vessel and its consciousness together can be polarized. This, along with its successful energizing, is the final step on the path of becoming an In-Perpetuum Being.~:~

~lumbering blindly
through life,
will nature forgive me?~

True compassion is exhibited when one shows compassion for a person's joy as well as his sorrow.

Chapter Eleven

Right Living
The Embodiment of Truth

**"A caterpillar sheds its skin
to find the butterfly within."**

.....it must be said, that behind all our inspiration and deep awakenings stand that "mysterious" spiritual energy of the Breath of Universal Life, which encourages us to continue on the Pure Mind Path, our chosen life practice, and transforms us as we go beyond, until we ourselves have matured into the object of our effort........................

Studying In-Perpetuum Beings one will begin to understand more fully the living practice dictated by Universal Nature. Knowing that these types of beings have existed for all time and therefore predate all religions, psychologies, and philosophies causes one to realize that they have no fixed dogma or religion, but are totally guided by the Breath of Universal Life. Through what we might label visions or awakenings, they naturally embody a life practice consistent with Universal Nature's tenets. Their living practice allows them to consciously bridge the chasm created by the human mind between the physical and spiritual worlds.

Perpetual Beings rely on inner knowledge to form conclusions about situations, rather than material or economic concerns which dictate intellectual and, therefore, inevitably wrong conclusions.

~:As In-Perpetuum Beings flowing in and out of physical form, they are fully aware that all elements of all the environments in and around all the universes are alive and contain life-sustaining energies. All life forms are interconnected and driven by the Breath of Universal Life. It is quite apparent then that all is dependent and mutually supportive and must be maintained in harmony and good health. Human beings must learn to understand this balance and learn to live in harmony with it, always setting aside ego in favor of all that is natural. The

Breath of Universal Life is the source of all power and knowledge from Universal Nature. Knowing and living its "Way" is the true source of all successful activities.~:~

One way Perpetual Beings access knowledge is through "awakening journeys." These journeys access the Breath's information by turning deeply inward while focusing on a question or problem. Answers are provided directly or indirectly depending on the degree of the meditative state. This method allows them the broader vision of Universal Nature as opposed to the dualistic intellectual mind.

~rising moon darkens,
black clouds o'
my shadow?~

Studying an In-Perpetuum Being is almost impossible unless you are his student. It is said that a student who doesn't understand his teacher's words, and possibly more important, doesn't understand the teacher's behavior itself is not a true student. Behavior is many times a better way of expressing one's meaning, clearly better than words. In Pure Mind practice we put an emphasis on behavior, not necessarily how to behave, but the natural expression of oneself. ~:When you listen to or observe a teacher you should give up all your subjective opinions; just listen and observe his "way." Listening without saying anything will give you the full meaning of what's being said, implied, or shown.~:~After all, what need be said?

~:Students embodying the Universal Life Wheel of Right Living know that with each step forward on this wondrous Pure Mind Path they rise *beyond,* for each and every step leads to the fulfillment of Universal Nature's call to awaken. Every movement of the student comprises (among other things):
—the personal manifestation of awakened knowledge,
—the avoidance of negative unwholesome factors in the future and the elimination of those which are present,
—wholly selfless giving,
—using the exertion of restraint, of overcoming, of maintaining, of developing the factors of awakening,
—striving to go beyond beliefs and convictions, though they were once of use to you, to Truth,
—continuous Pure Mind meditation practices,
—knowing that beliefs vary according to one's awakenings,
—mindfulness/living the present moment with the attitude of a pure spectator through which clear awakenings can be brought forth. The continuous practice of mindfulness brings one's mind

under control and allows one to choose either a state of rest, or states of vision, or states of contemplation, etc., depending on whether one is aiming for awakening, or insight into the Universal Nature of all existence (one of the bases of enlightenment), or for the creation of pure energy,
—striving to go beyond deceptive "inner experiences,"
—constant effort; showing endurance,
—burning any trace of self in each moment, and leaving no moments unfulfilled,
—"good will" or not having or performing any harmful thoughts or actions against any living thing,
—the avoidance of actions and thought that conflict with moral conduct dictated by Universal Nature,
—right livelihood—avoiding professions that are harmful to any sentient beings, i.e., hunter, narcotics, butcher, military, etc.,
—using good concentration in all endeavors,
—understanding not to rely on your own opinion, especially when judging your needs.~:~

~:The life practice of a Being In-Perpetuum or of a Pure Mind Path student involves much more and goes much deeper than just observing the lofty virtues as previously described. The prime essential is for the students' mental attitude to be solidly based on the recognition of Universal Nature, and they must know or see themselves as eternal Beings. They must accept the voidness of the ego, and their thoughts, words, and deeds must reflect these realizations. Practice divorced from right conduct, or practice and right conduct divorced from right attitude is totally useless.~:~

> ~a stalwart oak doesn't
> judge the woodpecker—
> how deep its roots?~

One of the ways we live our practice is to study, and one of the most important things we study is ourselves. We look at the makeup of our mind/body, what we think and how our thought processes work. Through study and practice we seek freedom, freedom from our fears, anxieties, desires, suffering, frustrations, and the like. We come to know that as we begin to comprehend how our ego minds operate, we can start to forget our ego selves and actually see that we can become the activity of existence or reality itself. When we reach this point satisfactorily, we start to reach for higher meanings beyond our physical existence, towards becoming an eternal being. It is also at this point that we truly start to enjoy our sentient existence.

chapter 11   Right Living

Awareness and awakening of the spiritual dimensions is an important purpose of this practice. It is designed to make students aware of their every moment so that they can live the meaning of life in their everyday activity, as Universal Nature meant it to be. ~:When we begin to understand and live correctly, we will be doing just what we should do. That is all! Nothing more. We awaken when it's time to awaken, we sit when it's time to sit, we work when it's time to work, we eat when it's time to eat, and always we create positive energy. Knowing the purpose of life, we come to understand that our life practice is nothing special, and so we feel nothing special. We just embody our practice, and that is man's purpose ~:~

"Outside" people looking at our spirituality, the simplicity of our life, the joy and happiness we radiate have a deep feeling of awe; but those who are practicing do not have this feeling. We can be likened to a sugar maple tree whose leaves are turning deep red with an autumn breeze dancing through our branches and the sun setting behind. To us this is just our life; we are just doing what we do, living our life standing there being a sugar maple. But those "outsiders" who are fortunate enough to have the time to stop and listen to the wind and feel the sun filtering through the maple's branches with its beautiful red leaves, always have a deep emotional feeling of awe; a few will possibly write a poem or two for the occasion. This is the way everything is.

~:To have good feelings about our practice is certainly not the point. Our disciplined life practice is not good or bad, hard or easy. Just like the sugar maple, we are doing exactly what Universal Nature tells us to do: fulfill our natures, nothing more and certainly nothing less.~:~

~look! look!
the wind is
stealing the leaves.~

~Inspiration
as the sun fades
along the hills
where the sugar maples
redden the horizon
sky I gaze beyond
to eternity, write
another poem still.~

Much of what Perpetual Beings have awakened and know can be seen in their character and the quality of life they live. When searching for a teacher/guide or just to *observe right living practice,* it would be well to understand what they know and how they manifest it. In-Perpetuum Beings move in and out and through levels of consciousness in a flash and at their will. They handle change easily because of their ability to adapt in spiritual as well as ordinary states of consciousness. They are quite comfortable with things that seem unbelievable, yet may be true. They are not intellectual philosophers but awakened practitioners. Their knowledge of the Breath of Universal Life and how to communicate with it teaches them how all the energies in the universe work and how to use them. Recognizing the inherent power in all nature and their connection with it manifests in moral behavior. They can live and practice outside of ritual and have no "religious" articles of worship. Through meditation practice they have learned how to relax their physical bodies so that they become more receptive and efficient. They are able to quiet their minds so that they can receive and comprehend awakenings. Using tools of imagination, when they first start meditation practice they are able to envision and journey to various places for the knowledge and vital information necessary to see any evolution state in order to qualify other latent possibilities. "All visible comes from invisible reality." They show no mystical aura and will not perform "magic tricks." They know how to laugh, because they can detach themselves from the human condition and, therefore, find it amusing. They know not to judge situations or events but just to trust their inner self. They refuse to place any significance on modern day commentaries of classic texts. They know how to understand people and how to help them towards healing. They also have great insight into all living beings. Their ability to communicate internally as well as externally at the same time keeps them in both worlds simultaneously. They are, therefore, in touch with both and do not lose track of either. They are aware that the human mind is limited in scope and a hindrance to understanding beyond the known to the unknown. They will not produce an atmosphere of power to prove anything. Looking at the life of a Perpetual Being you see the "Way" of Universal Nature manifested by their right living practice.

> **~:Into In-Perpetuum Beings
> wisdom flows unhindered.~:~**

> ~When you leave the
> animals to their seasons,
> and the flowers
> to blow in the wind,
> you sow the
> seeds of compassion.~

> ~dry summer wind
> forcing native grasses
> to dance.~

In order to teach the elements of a right living practice, we must address the true nature of defilements, attachments, dualistic thinking, and other inner dangers for the purpose of their elimination and/or separation. These things provide no true happiness or spiritual gain.

~:Since defilements come from clinging to things, we start with understanding the aggregates of attachment, because if you're successful in separating the aggregates from clinging, you will separate yourself from defilement. The most common aggregates of attachments are: emotion, body, will, memory through perception, and consciousness.~:~

Emotion (feeling)—impermanence is too quickly forgotten when pain and pleasure arise. We easily overlook the fact that they are not Self, so we identify with them and thus are tortured by these misunderstandings.

Physical form (body)—not accepting aging, decay, and the eventual death of our bodies; its constant prey to illness and pain when it is not in harmony with our desires; and when we feel attraction or repulsion towards the bodies of others, we have grief, sorrow, and we suffer a great deal. One or all of these factors can rob us of any true peace.

Will—the imposing of our preferences. When we do not understand the nature of mental states, we react, sometimes violently, causing our thoughts and feelings, likes and dislikes, happiness and sorrows to arise, and forgetting that they are impermanent and Selfless, we cling to them.

Memories and perceptions—we identify with what we recognize and this almost always gives rise to hatred, greed, and/or delusion. Our wrong perceptions and understandings become habitual, strongly imbedded in our subconscious.

Consciousness—we hold tightly onto the self that befriends the other aggregates. We think, "I know, I am, I feel," and are bound by the illusion of "self," or separation.

~:When all or any of these attachments are incorrectly understood they lead to wrong action. Our goal is to understand and let go of these things so as not to cling to "me or mine." These aggregates of attachments have a potential for great harm and will not disappear, so we must simply not grasp them as our own. Those few who understand the impermanence of these things and practice accordingly come to know all the great joys.~:~

~:Attachments, one of the "inner dangers," rob us of our freedom and ultimately destroy us. Our senses bring the things to us that cause lust, anger, compulsion, and ignorance to arise. These things have the power to destroy the love, compassion, and kindness in us. Defilements caused by emotion

chapter 11 — Right Living

can bury our True Nature beneath an insurmountable pile of illusions. Last, but not least, are greed and hatred which continually bring us anguish; lust and aversion which cause us to speak and do wrong; delusions which lead us to see good as bad, ugly as beautiful, valueless as valuable. Those who do not live the Pure Mind Path do not see.~:~

We strive for a practice that is undefiled, and in order to accomplish something even close to that state, we must first eliminate the most pertinent defilements. ~:The defilements which almost immediately negate most of the previously created or gathered energies are: knowingly killing or abusing or causing to be killed or abused any living sentient being either physically, verbally, or with thought projection; any attempt, realized or not, to disrupt a community or its teachers; stealing, lying, gossiping, or any such deceitful practice. And if one's life practice does not remain well intended and properly interwoven with the conduct and attitudes that constitute the basis of this practice, it will bear the consequences of defilement.~:~

Chapter Twelve

Awakening the Unknown

*Wisdom being immortal
does not die with man,
it continues to flow unhindered.*

m a

When the practitioner
is ready, awakening
masters appear..........

chapter 12 Awakening the Unknown

~:Awakened enlightenment is not something to talk about, but something to practice in your life.~:~

The deep enlightenment of Universal Nature cannot be described in words, terms of doctrine, or forms of ceremony. Doctrine needs only small amounts of teaching, ritual ceremony needs only obedience and repetition, and words cannot express the two sides of truth, positive and negative, so we cannot express the whole truth in one word. *~:Universal Nature is something which is in creation itself, not something which results from creation.*

Awakenings are at most times expressed by their embodiment and cannot be figured out by logic. So enlightenment is something we express by our activities, our joy, and our enjoyment of the moment. Awakenings can be very complicated to describe, very simple to experience, and we still cannot figure them out. ~:~Yet understanding enlightenment at any depth becomes rather simple when you practice the Universal Life Wheel and in particular, its meditation techniques, though these techniques are not enlightenment itself.

Enlightenment cannot be attained by another's words or by conceptualizing. "Be your own lamp."
Buddha

~:Enlightening moments, in which one momentarily awakens to some or all Truths of Universal Nature, are direct and unmeditated experiences, almost always attained by those devoted to a true inner path. ~:~Contrary to popular belief, this is not brought about by visions, drugs, hypnosis, ecstasy, voodoo, dancing, whirling, praying, meditation techniques, kundalini, or any other "paths" claimed by various religions, cults, New Agers, and the like.

~:Awakening Truth lies in total submission of the human will and intellect. Furthermore, the student or disciple applies rigorous self-discipline in preparation for these mystical experiences.~:~ The unanimous descriptions of reincarnate "mystics" such as all Buddhas, Jesus Christ, St. Theresa of Avila, St. John of the Cross, Gandhi, etc., together with the manifest intellectual and "moral" qualities shown by these people, make it impossible to doubt or reject this Path out of hand as mere delusion.

Why would reincarnates choose to live again in any form only to become tainted by that form's nature with the possibility of losing the state of InPerpetuum? ~:Know that they begin to recover their pure integrity with Universal Nature's call to turn back inward. They become purer and purer as they go deeper and deeper beyond their humanity. After they recreate their energy essence vehicle, as it was before returning to form, and when they release from the mind/body and the material world with its perplexities and suffering, Eternal and Perpetual Beings totally recover their pure innate integrity.

When you awaken the unknown you're in a spiritual dimension. Spirituality shines because you have been deeply inspired, touched, and penetrated by Universal Nature. You embody the universal aspects of reality beyond man's nature, and you characterize its highest moral quality.

When it comes to spirituality, words cannot convey its message. It is a phenomenon that is inexpressible.~:~ When you hear the dawn sounds of awakening creatures, you cannot express the meaning or the feeling of it through words. You can be judgmental, saying it was "good" or "bad," but that doesn't convey anything. As when walking in the desert and seeing a beautiful flower in the midst of arid sands, you can say it is beautiful, but those words will never convey the actual realization of the moment, because they will be interpreted according to the listener's experiences. A person who has never seen nor felt the beauty and the depth of that particular moment might understand the words without understanding anything at all.

~:Spiritual awakenings are so infinite, so precise and impeccable, so silent that trying to express them in language destroys them. Spiritual things cannot be conveyed, because words confine things into a very narrow sphere and most of their meaning is lost.~:~

Science, physics, mathematics can be conveyed and therefore taught. But in the realm of ideas and emotions, the more you try to convey the more you "feel" like your words have left something behind. Like giving someone an empty can, they hold the container without the contents. A moment between mother and child—how is it possible to convey that feeling to another person?

~:There is reason which is wholly expressible; there are emotions and they are expressible to a point beyond which they become inexpressible; and finally there's spirituality, which is absolutely inexpressible. Spirituality, therefore, cannot be taught.~:~

~ego dimmed,
integrity intact—
my self reappeared~

Awakenings are limitless, so there will be no definitive way to end this record while Mahan Agass remains in physical form, except to say that when a devoted practitioner of Pure Mind Practice passes out of physical form, there is a beginning.

~:Embodying by living the lofty pure Universal Life Wheel, the student has cleansed himself of all hindrances through calming his desires, passions, and most importantly, negating his ego. This practice opens the heart/mind to the never ending influx of intuitive wisdom. By advancing onward, the student fully experiences the state of consciousness which rises moment by moment and beyond this to the state of pure non-dualistic thought, a "oneness" with the energies and the essence that flows in and around all things.~:~

~:Reading or hearing these words avails one absolutely nothing. *It is only the undefiled experience of it that liberates, awakens, and enlightens.* Students who send forth their minds to dwell in silence day after day, night after night, year after year cease to be as other beings. Their personalities, thoughts, words, and deeds are saturated through and through with the brilliance of non-attachment consciousness as they approach the state of an In-Perpetuum Being. Into them wisdom flows unhindered. Theirs alone is the honor that comes with this mighty achievement, provided that their thoughts, deeds, and practice remain well intended and properly interwoven with the conduct, attitude, and morality which constitute the Pure Mind Path and Universal Nature.~:~

Awakening the Unknown

Awakening experiences are the equivalent of a spiritual education which, for the most part, is not attainable through a structured, dictatorial system. In modern-day religions a student is conditioned to confuse many basic premises of spiritual growth. Accepting deceptive premises, he sees himself as learning, because he is being taught; he sees the upward advancement in a church's hierarchy as spiritual attainment; he believes with the publishing of a text he has said or created something new and significant; he sees being educated to perform a service, such as teaching, as having value. These and many more poorly conceived premises are allowed to continue, because people have an overwhelming "hunger" for spiritual growth. Religion's basic premises, for the most part, do not incorporate Universal Nature's tenets, and therefore cannot begin to fulfill a person's basic desire for spiritual growth beyond simple low level awakenings.

As a result of a few minor awakenings and multitudinous self-indulgent books, religion is able to justify its existence. It can and often does deceive most of society by claiming as its value its ability to serve man in his search and his attainment of spiritual enlightenment. With the illusion of spiritual advancement many religions have deceived society into financing its institutions. It is under the guise of spirituality that religion claims freedom from taxation and society's laws. It is while under the protection of these ill-conceived laws that religion allocates more and more of its tax-free dollars to *management and facilities,* which may be seen as its true underlying purpose given its lack of any true spiritual understanding or practice.

Although a seeker's awakenings can be enhanced and sped up by only a very few religious institutions, nevertheless the seeker's attainment should not be judged by his institution's religious affiliation, its teachers, religious texts, robes of rank, diplomas, rite of passage ceremonies, or dharma transmissions. Every education, spiritually inspired or attained by formal education, should be linked and judged by a student's embodiment and practice of that education. Most certainly, spiritual growth should not and cannot be judged by symbols attainable by approved and/or condoned measures under religion's or society's control.

~on and on,
human voices—
yesterday's conquests,
tomorrow's hopes—
all wasted moments.~

~traveling beyond—
leaving behind city walls;
all wild creatures
welcome this stranger~

~Oh In-Perpetuum Being,
what deep mysteries
lie beyond your smile?~

Chapter Thirteen

Energy in Relation to Motion and Space

Our practice binds each to each and we become one breath.

~Empty of all except this moment.~

chapter 13 — Energy, Motion & Space

~:Any latent possibility energized by an In-Perpetuum Energy Being reveals itself in two fundamental ways: as motion, and as that in which motion takes place, namely space. This space can be seen as a window with a curtain, because it is through the curtain that all things, either physical or an extension of same (thought), step into visible appearance. As that which comprises all things, a sentient being exists in a three-dimensional space of form, sense perception, and thought (memory and abstract), and in this capacity is called human. The nature of space, however, is not limited to three dimensions: it includes all possibilities of movement, not only the physical and mental, but also the spiritual movement which comprises infinite dimensions. You should, therefore, understand that turning inward to the spiritual dimensions can put you on a much higher plane of existence. The human being is in an infancy phase of his evolution which makes it difficult to recognize and/or understand the spirituality of which he is capable.~:~

~:The plane of spiritual activity is called "the spiritual dimension of consciousness." When one reaches the highest stage of this consciousness, a state where duality of object and subject is eliminated, he enters the Universal Nature Dimension. This state of awareness goes beyond the human and all other natures that are tied to behavior and form.~:~

chapter 13 *Energy, Motion & Space*

For the sake of communication we can refer to the environment or medium that comprises the space in which motion takes place as "smoke-like," a light and airy gaseous condition. It is within this smoke-space, no matter its form, that energy movement creates vibrations. ~:However, the principle of movement can only be understood by knowing its prime mover which is the Breath of Universal Life. This Breath is the all-powerful, all-pervading rhythm of Universal Nature which directs the course of all things in every dimension, including the suns and their planets. We can equate this movement to the inhalation and exhalation of the human body which maintains the circulation of blood and the currents of psychic energy. All forces of the universe, including those of the human mind, from the highest consciousness to the depths of the subconscious, are modifications of Universal Breath. Unlike the human breath not all breath is physical. With the human species, breathing is the only way they can live, but a human's breath is only one of many functions through which universal and primordial energy force manifests itself.~:~

~:In the highest sense, as Einstein discovered, motion and space cannot be separated, because they determine each other like above and below, or right and left. It is only possible to see and distinguish the influences of the one to the other in the realm of practical experience.

All that is formed and occupies a position in space by possessing some aggregate reveals the nature of space. Therefore, the four great elements or states of aggregation, namely solid, liquid, heat (fire), and gas (air) are seen as modifications of this space (as defined earlier).~:~

~:All dynamic qualities that cause movement, change, or transformation reveal the nature of the Breath of Life from Universal Nature. All bodily or psychic processes, all physical or spiritual forces, including breathing, circulation of blood, activity of the nervous system, as well as mental activities and higher spiritual functions are modifications of the Breath of Universal Life.~:~

Smoke-like space in one form presents itself as matter, in another form it merges without perception into the realm of spiritual dynamic forces. For example, the aggregate state of fire is material as well as energy; similarly, the In-Perpetuum Being may exist in the mental and spiritual dimensions of consciousness, and higher yet, in the Universal Nature dimension of consciousness, all at the same moment. The Universal Breath, on the other hand, also appears in such bodily functions as breathing, digestion, etc., and is the source of physical and psychic energy.

~:The interaction of body and mind, of spiritual

and material forces, of matter and consciousness, sense-organs and sense-objects, is totally dependent upon the Universal Life Breath to function. Without it that interaction would be impossible. It is precisely this interaction which we make use of, and upon where the techniques of our Pure Mind meditation are grounded.~:~

~:The body and mind are the instruments we have for the awakening of Universal Nature. Any turning away from this physical life is a turning away from the completeness of Universal Nature Wisdom and a renunciation of its aim in an earthly human embodiment. Therefore we must not ignore the body-mind for they are indispensable to a perfect spirituality and the achievement of an In-Perpetuum state.~:~

The study of human physiology systems and their centers of cosmic forces, their flow and/or their dammed up condition, is not, in fact, necessary to the understanding of this level of awakening experience. You might wish to know, however, ~:that the practitioners who control these cosmic forces reach, through them, the highest spiritual power and perfection while those who do not control them and therefore ignorantly release or misuse them are, in turn, destroyed by them.~:~

Just as cosmic forces can be utilized for benefit or

chapter 13 — Energy, Motion & Space

destruction, so can the forces which reside in the human body lead to liberation or bondage, towards the awakening light or into the darkness of form and energy dissipation.

~:Only with perfect concentration, self control, and clear knowledge of the nature of these forces should a being dare to use them. Because the directions for a human to awaken are only correctly interpreted by and, therefore, communicated (whether in spiritual writings, orally, or mentally transmitted) by a reincarnated In-Perpetual Being, only those who have been instructed by a reincarnate can understand and perform right life practice and meditation.~:~

The perceived veil of secrecy covering these esoteric teachings is, in fact, deliberate. It is not aimed at preventing others from awakening such powers or knowledge, ~:but at protecting the ignorant from the dangers and misuse of experimentation with these practices. The Pure Mind practice with its Perpetual Life Wheel recognizes and intentionally avoids these dangers by its pace of movement and awakenings.~:~

~:The power of the Perpetual Life Wheel is revealed depending on whether or not there is a good and moral effort. Clear perception depends upon its continuous practice.~:~

~doubts
do not water
a garden~

~an empty vessel,
whispering, poetic lines,
past lives!~

~mountains pierce the sky,
butterflies kissing flowers,
I'm lost again.~

Part Three

The Answers
Most Frequently Sought

~My mind cleansed
of useless junk—
what to put back?~

.

Wisdom does not
arise from ego desire;
simply let go!

Part three   *Questions and Answers*

Most questions asked of enlightened beings are nonsense. Intellectual and metaphysical questions are for verbal knowledge, not for authentic practice and living. One should ask questions that lead to, or are concerned with, the spiritual and inner dimensions. The intellect is our connection to the "outside," to the material world. So answers to such questions never lead to the inner spiritual dimensions nor provide anything meaningful in helping you become a Perpetual Being.

Questions and answers can become a vicious cycle, always spinning on the periphery; the heart is never reached. Have you ever noticed that most questions ask about something, especially about self. But knowing about yourself is not knowing you, so you gather much knowledge about things and never truly know or experience them.

When you choose to ask a question, ask one that will aid in deepening your practice for this is what your future and present lives depend upon. Try to ask questions that are of the very moment you are in, a "now" question. When you ask such a question, it is a step towards personal freedom. Furthermore, questions whose answers will not change you in any way are meaningless. Example: How many planets throughout the universe support sentient life? What difference will the answer make to you? How will the answer change your life or help you with your practice? On the other hand, if the answers you seek will change you or your practice, then they become very meaningful. Questions should also come from the immediate moment, spontaneously. If no questions arise and all you feel is deeply silent, that is ideal.

~:Alas, only a few who question and study truly want to practice. Most want to study and know in an intellectual way. This is totally meaningless in a spiritual practice of importance.~:~

> ~moments without
> thought, I need
> no introduction~
>
> ~adrift
> seeking nothing
> moon drops glisten~

Most modern day religions have an approximate date of "birth." How old is the practice of which you speak?

Prior to the practice itself making an appearance here on Earth, In-Perpetuum Beings either existed in a form other than human or visited through the means of animal forms. For more information about how this is accomplished refer back to chapter ten "Life As an In-Perpetuum Being."

Part three *Questions and Answers*

About three to five hundred years after combining evolutionary forces created the human species as we know it today, the first In-Perpetuum Universal Being was reincarnated as a human on this planet. It was at the point of his turning inward to re-awaken that Pure Mind practice, as it is called today, first appeared here. You can recognize that it has been with us for many millions of years, and though the practice itself has undergone many name changes, it remains basically the same. Because this practice is under the direct guidance of Universal Nature, it will remain unblemished throughout all Universal cycles. It can be no other way.

The practice has appeared in many forms, in all countries, and deep within some religions. Those reincarnates who turned to a religious practice as a means of reawakening transcended that religion's boundaries in short order. Through their enlightening experiences they were able to identify the one true practice. Though comparatively a minute percentage of humans, In-Perpetuum Beings were and are many in number and are of all races, faiths, and most live in this world unrecognized by those who do not see. And yet all of humanity is affected by their work and powerful presence.

Are there other books or scholars I can consult on the subject of becoming In-Perpetuum?

Until this record is printed, the only other sources of these truths *in total* are through your own very deep awakening guided by an In-Perpetuum reincarnated teacher. This is a record of one In-Perpetuum Being's awakening to the necessity of furthering the evolution of humanity to a place where awakenings are made easier and becoming eternal is made possible. Because we are at a point in the Universal Cycle's evolution where the energizing of a greater number of latent possibilities is taking place, an almost doubling of the percentage of In-Perpetuum Beings must also take place. This will require, in earth time, quite a long period, but in comparison to time-space reality it's just a blink of the eye. The human species is evolved only to the point where their conscious mind makes it difficult, if not nearly impossible, to awaken deeply and transcend the known. With the keys of Pure Mind practice and its Universal Life Wheel it becomes a matter of "doing, being, and receiving."There are relatively few In-Perpetuum Beings, especially teacher/guides, in physical form on Earth. Chances of finding one are minuscule and depend greatly upon your level of practice and pure energy that can invoke the law of attraction.

~Pure Mind Path:
in a meadowlark's song
I hear my teacher's voice.~

Part three   Questions and Answers

If teachers or mentors are so crucial, why are they not readily available to most seekers?

In-Perpetuum Beings in physical form carry out many functions of evolutionary "shifts" or corrections. Many do not have teaching as a mission. Those who do carry a mission of teaching are not available to just any seeker. From this specific question, for example, it is clear that you have an attitude of self-importance, that you believe that an individual is the most important thing for us to be concerned with. Know and understand that we do not exist to lead humans to awakening. ~:The great need for a teacher shows itself clearly when the student does not perceive his need.~:~

What is the Universal Cycle?

Everything within the universe, including the universe itself, begins and ends. To try and picture the Universal Cycle, it's best to start at its ending. One moment just before the cycle ends, all physical and thought phenomena that have existed and evolved come to their natural passing. There remains nothing of possibility that has not been or is not at the present time existing, all having been energized into existence. Along with the human being which has evolved to its final highly spiritual stage, most possibilities have come and gone and are completely known. At this point *everything* comes to its natural end, dissipates, and nothing remains, not even the memory of all that existed, for at this moment there is no mind with remembrances. The one vital exception is a single In-Perpetuum Being submerged in a myriad of latent possibilities, sharing with Universal Nature but one thought, that of knowing their natures, their physical embodiment, their evolution etc., and most important, the understanding that Universal Nature permeates all things. And so with the energizing of one possibility, the cycle starts over. Each new cycle brings with it no predestined plan or map to follow. All of them evolve differently, but they have the same tendencies so that they parallel each other closely.

~Oh my!
I'm sitting in
midst of nothing.~

Can you explain the similarity of near-death experiences that people claim to have had?

The descriptions I have heard are very close to the actual events of passing out of form, though there is a monumental difference between the passing of In-Perpetuum Beings and the rest of humanity. As In-Perpetuum Beings die, their remaining energies gather in what has been called throughout this book their energy vessel. The rest of humanity's energies just release from their cells and flow out of one or all of the nine points of exit.* This, of course, includes the mind's energies stored as memory. As life slips away, the memory energies leave the cells and present all beings with a very quick glimpse of their whole lives. This is the reason we can say, "Our whole life passed before us." Our fond remembrances of other people and experiences naturally contain the strongest energies.

For the In-Perpetuum Being, his energy vessel continues to gather near what Western science calls the "mysterious gland" and what most mystics, adepts, etc. from the East know as the "third eye." As this energy gathers it gets brighter and brighter until it reaches a point of white brilliant light. When his mind/body ceases functioning, his energy vessel leaves the body and the "third eye," which is still functioning, sees this important event in its usual spectator role.

The rest of humanity's third eye with its bright light also awakens at this juncture and observes their energy's departure through the other exit points. In either case, if their mind/body starts to function again, or as you say "returns to life," then the energy package is forced to reverse and is drawn back through the third eye gland. It is here that we find the explanation of "I found myself walking towards a bright light." Actually, it was inward, but there is no way for the mind to know that.

*See The Final Life Moment in chapter 10

Here, also, we find the explanation for the people from their past who were waiting or calling or pointing or urging them on into the light. These are the strong memory energies that are returning with the rest of the energies to their former cells. It is also here that we possibly find the loss of some memory and/or motor skills experienced by a few, for some of their memory energies might have dissipated before returning. The reason "returning to life" for "general humanity" must take place within a relatively short time is that if the energy package moves too far away, there's not enough energy left in the mind/body to reverse its course and it will dissipate.

Here with the bright light of the third eye and the movement of energy we can find the explanation for the sightings of "souls leaving the body" and in some notable cases rising to heaven.

Very powerful adepts can perform feats of levitation by gathering and directing these same energies downward outside the body and lifting the body upward. Astral travel and mind over matter feats are also performed by projecting energies outward. As explained previously, In-Perpetuum Beings consider these feats defilements of their life's practice due to the wasteful use of important energies which are difficult enough to garner and will be lost to them and their purpose forever.

> ~passing away
> his thoughts
> were full of life~

How should humans judge the meaning of their lives?

Almost all humans conduct and judge their lives only as their lives are seen by others. They dress, think, talk, and live in accord with their society, parents, peers, and desires. Without other people to judge by or to be judged by, they would have no egos, no identity, for what would they identify with? Without something to relate to there could be no color, no race, no gender, no good, no evil, no style, no fat nor thin, no civilization, no laws, no standards, no need for Gods; we would just appear and disappear. There would be no judgment and, in their eyes, no meaning.

One of the secondary forces that drives human sentient beings to this practice is the search for a meaningful life beyond the judgment of other people. With the awakening to the truth of impermanence, they begin to understand that all form is transitory including themselves. Moment to moment nothing remains as it was nor as one would have it be. Neither our eyes nor our minds can see or know the momentary changes as they take place. Do you see each and every hair on your head turning gray? In fact your hair, your blood cells, your thoughts, and all other physical aggregates that are your being and everything else throughout all the universe are never the same from one moment to the next. So humans may begin to see that they are not the same person at this moment as they were a moment ago. A person's life, if it is to be judged, can only be judged on a momentary basis. Unless one turns inward, for whatever reason, life just comes and goes **and it's only in the minds of the people they left behind that their life had meaning.** It is very hard on the ego to accept that our lives only have meaning based on the judgment of other humans. Unfortunately ego desire is the wrong reason to turn inward for meaning and, therefore, can never succeed.

~without a mirror
one can rejoice
anytime.~

Isn't my nature different from yours? If not, how do you understand the word nature?

Basically I use the word in two different ways. First, Nature is the principle and/or power that dictates and guides the natural essence of existence for all phenomena and its creation, as in Universal Nature. Second, individual natures are the overall system or pattern of particular objects or forces such as solar systems, planets, humans, animals, plants, etc., as in human nature.

Humans have a tendency to use nature as rationalization for their behavior. It is never their nature to do something that is in direct violation of Universal Nature's laws. It is because it is in their nature to have choices that they are able to create or accept many flaws in their thinking and character. By not understanding the natural way of things, man makes terrible decisions affecting the lives of all phenomena on earth including his own. By destroying his ability to become eternal and, therefore, his purpose for being, he takes away his only chance for true peace, joy, and happiness.

People look around at other people and see differences both physical and mental. They see that each person possesses a unique personality and character. Unfortunately they see these differences as each one's own nature. There is no question that each sentient being has its own idiosyncrasies, talents, and abilities. However, a human's nature itself does not occur at random; it is the nature of all humanity.

Character traits much like belief systems are, knowingly or not, created or adopted. When correctly understood by man a tree is a tree, a bird is a bird, and a Universal Truth is Truth beyond his definition. Using trees as an example we can see how they differ one from the other even within the same species. Looking deeper we see that even on the same tree each leaf is different in color, shape, and size, but each stems from the same root, and like all humans who stem from the same root nature, that nature is permeated by Universal Nature and that cannot change.

As man evolves, his clarity of seeing will evolve and his purpose of being and the laws of all Natures will become known to him. As this is happening he will make fewer and fewer wrong decisions that affect him, the planet, and the universe.

Other than the obvious long-term benefits of this practice, are there any advantages in the present life?

There are many, starting with the realization that you are in charge of your life and can throw away the "victim of circumstances" attitude that most people have. You might even feel inspired by obstacles that you were previously incapable of handling, but now you're capable of doing so. You'll have the capability of tapping into universal energies. Your thoughts about how events in your life are shaped will change. For example, your thinking about linear time will be altered, providing you with much more freedom. Your understanding of the real powers that exist will help enhance your experiences. Your insight into compassion will put your relationships on a far different level and your communication skills will improve. You will begin to understand how you are connected to all of life. No longer feeling separate, your perspective broadens. You will understand how to be in touch with knowledge you didn't think possible. You will undergo radical transformation the closer you get to the true nature of reality. You will become more relaxed and have virtually no stress especially in the face of perceived adversity. You will learn never to allow the events in your life to bind you, but also not to withdraw from them. You will come to think tomorrow's thoughts when tomorrow comes. You will know, understand, and appreciate that worldly feelings are not sublime.

Turning inward, does one have to take a vow of poverty?

Living simply without the burden of possessions is quite necessary, but the major things we all must give up or let go of are our ego and our dualistic ideas. Thinking dualistically and egotistically keeps us separate from everything else that exists. When you give up the idea of separateness, there is no distinction between man and woman, sky and earth, teacher and disciple, etc., and you find the true meaning of being. You make no value judgments, because everything has the same value, so when your senses come into contact with something, it is just as it is, nothing more or less. You give each thing the same respect by understanding that all are the same. Not feeling separate is a very serious part of our practice and very necessary for a successful conclusion. Not seen as separate from the rest of nature, you begin to realize true knowledge and evoke deep awakenings. At best, elimination of self-centered ideas is difficult, but the effort will help appease your innermost desire to awaken. A true Pure Mind Path student embraces the whole of the universes without labels.

The delight of being in union with Universal Nature is sweeter than any material riches or fulfilled desires.

~no moon tonight
the sky dropped it
in my mind.~

Are teachers and prophets of other disciplines likely to be reincarnated?

These prophets, seers, teachers, gurus, etc., can become eternal only if their practice recognizes and encompasses all that is dictated by Universal Nature and thereby attracts an In-Perpetuum teacher of their own. Otherwise, they will continue to live only in the minds, hearts, and words of their students. As with most of humanity, their physical and mental energies disperse upon their passing. In contrast, In-Perpetuum reincarnates live an eternal and infinite life. Their lives are sustained by their deeds, thoughts, and reawakening practice which are solely guided by Universal Nature. Their Pure Mind practice congeals their energy with all that's infinite. Their everyday deeds, teaching, and their correction adjustments of evolution can be seen wherever you look and will be understood whenever you raise your consciousness.

Meeting an In-Perpetuum teacher, what should one's aim be?

If and when you meet a reincarnate teacher, try to see what cannot be seen, hear his unspoken words, try to experience with him the elation of awakening, the revelation of Universal Nature, the inspiration of awe, selfless giving, and love. This teacher is a guide on a path of high consciousness, liberation, compassion, patience, love, and is the one true source of pure practice in human form. Unify your mind with his, and you'll achieve and receive.

If, after studying with a teacher for a while, he were to pass on, who will guide my practice?

If your mirror's dirt has been removed and the dust

has settled, the images will remain clear. If your heart is pure, then all things in your world will be pure....then the sun, the moon, the trees, the flowers, as well as birds and animals will guide you along the way. If this is not the case and you are worthy of the practice, an In-Perpetuum teacher will be attracted to you.

"Be grateful to one who urges you to return to your difficult spiritual practice, no matter what their motivation seems to be. Most offer comfort and an easy path and it is those you must worry about."

I have become totally confused with the use of the word enlightenment; can you clarify its meaning?

Enlightenment is a spiritual state of awakening. Unfortunately there are no words to describe this ungraspable experience. Trying to reduce to words what is conceptually impossible to the human mind is laughable, at best. Enlightenment is not a concept. When experiencing it there is no separation, therefore there is no object to see nor subject to experience it. Where the word enlightenment is used in the sutras and commentaries, it should be viewed as a shallow experience that needs to grow deeper. Enlightenment is a word mainly used to impress others. The more words used to describe and embellish the experience, the more you can believe that the speaker has never experienced it.

You must beware of the intellectual approach of those who hang on to words and ask you to believe in these words rather than demanding that you experience directly their deeper meaning. Due to the workings of human minds at this stage in their evolution, they can only communicate the relative truths of the phenomenal world or their delusions in opposition to Universal Nature's ultimate truth which can be experienced and then communicated in a spiritual dimension.

~tattered patchwork pillow,
an eternal being
sits beyond limitations.~

Most of the hierarchy in the popular world religions are very exposed, very available. Why do In-Perpetuum Beings conceal themselves?

Anyone who is open to the high spiritual dimensions becomes aware of us and recognizes the spiritual energy that emanates from our presence. Many mystics function secretly. Some seek isolation, away from the "maddening crowd." But whether they go into the mountains, monasteries, forests or caves, their silence is telling, their energies are highly visible, and their work easily recognized. But most seekers are not open and their awareness level is low. However, the true answer would be, what would be the point? We are not trying to convert or convince anyone.

You have said many times that logical thought is a barrier to contact with spiritual dimensions and understandings; can you give me an example this? Logic dictates that one cannot be the many and the one at the same time or vice versa, but while in a spiritual dimension one experiences clearly, and in no uncertain terms, that the one is multiform while yet remaining one. Applying many different contradictory levels of awakened knowledge to a singular event, experience, or being can be made very apparent. There are times when it is convenient to view things as independent, other times as an illusion, and yet other times when it is best to recognize them as void. Logic is useless in the attempt to reach a spiritual state and in spiritual affairs.

Can you express to me in words your experiences and feelings about the Pure Mind Path's Life Practice?

Impossible! But for the sake of this record it can be described through the eyes of a student. The Pure Mind Path is a very deep and undefiled practice which is the perfection of all that (Universal Nature) which is truly perfect. Our life itself is a wondrous practice that is most rare, and for the first time it is being revealed to all, thereby solving for us the previously hidden and profoundest mystery of all awakened ones. It guides us to the "nowness" of our need to awaken, thereby enabling us to comprehend the Truth of Universal Nature, and its need for us to become an Eternal Being, In-Perpetuum. It also shows us that there is no other wholly awakened life than the Pure Mind Path way of living.

This life practice dictated by Universal Nature is a pure and wondrous way of being and becoming. By sitting in a joyous serene silence, awakening the qualities of Universal Nature, and further manifesting them by our deeds and thoughts, we reach a union with all things, all natures, and ourselves. Experiencing and understanding the true meaning of life, and the fact that it has merit, and we as humans can indeed play an important role in the universal scheme if we choose to, is a momentous realization moment. We learn that eternal life or eternal nothingness is in our choosing and this energizes us to stay with our practice moment by moment, day by day, year by year, aeon by aeon. By being on the true path of the Universal Nature way, we know to live our whole lives as our practice, and not just to fit our practice somewhere in our lives.

Pure Mind practice also teaches us to be very patient; after cultivating our minds and planting the seeds we leave the matter of our awakening to the nature of the Breath of Universal life, for there is nothing else we can do. We understand that we cannot dictate to any nature, so if it takes one or one hundred and one years to awaken fully, we are at peace and do not suffer from expectation.

You speak of different energy groups. Do any of these fall into what people refer to as the spirit world?

One of the basic awakenings of students is the knowledge that energy underlies all life. What I believe people are referring to is our contact with spiritual energy that is the source power for all life and is directly related to each form's nature. Ordinary people see the world as a physical environment that operates according to physical laws, with a certain order but no meaning. For the Perpetual Being, as well as advanced students of the Pure Mind Path, the Breath of Universal Life, which carries Universal Nature energy, proves the coherency of all forms and gives meaning to life. Without the greater universal energy there would be chaos. The Breath of Universal Life energy is not a theory or a figure of speech but a definite reality that is as fundamental as breathing or thinking. For students, the awakening knowledge of this energy power propels them into mastery of their lives. Understanding the physical world of form and its energies is a good mental exercise, but is in no way adequate for understanding our underlying Nature and, therefore, does not provide the keys that are essential to truly understanding anything spiritual.

The Universal Breath remains hidden to all people until they unveil it. Having done so, the wisdom beyond all known wisdom and the energy powers become available and clear to them. But like most jewels, they are difficult to unveil, and it may take a very long time to do so. If a student keeps "polishing his mirror," he removes the crust and dust, and lo and behold a jewel is found.

Consider where the In-Perpetuum Being's mind goes to see this knowledge. To you, when you see a rock, it's a rock; the wind is moving air, animals are sentient beings, and humans are the same with higher mental abilities and emotions. Living or not, when you dissect the human or all other forms, they are just smaller pieces of the same. Take them down further and they are atoms made up of the same basic materials as all other forms. Go further still, and they are particle waves mostly in what we call "space smoke." At this level science becomes totally confused, having no understanding within and beyond the subatomic level. This is where we spend most of our time. Here is where the same underlying Universal energy that is within all animals, humans, rocks, trees, wind, water, and every other form both animate and inanimate resides.

Here also is where we can communicate with the Breath of Universal Nature and all other species and forms. It is here that one gains a deep understanding and respect for Universal Nature as well as the ever-evolving natures of all things. Real power comes from knowledge, and that is why it is not available to ordinary people who have no respect for the workings of Universal Nature.

I have heard the expression "clear seeing" as a way to understand "suchness or itness." Could you explain it further?

There are so many phrases and words used in attempts to communicate mindful or awakening experiences. We use the phrase "as-it-isness" in our attempt to communicate seeing a thing clearly, or our "oneness" experience with that thing. When you look at something or someone and really see "all" there is to see, then it sees you in the same manner. It is at this juncture that it is no longer just it, and you are no longer just you. You and it dissolve into something way beyond where it can be explained logically, but we definitely experience it. To bring about and perfect this intuitive wisdom requires opening ourselves up and being mindful at the same time. That is clear seeing. But if you attempt to bring any selfish motives to the experience, it will not work.

Part three *Questions and Answers* 23

Are all the rituals necessary for a spiritual practice to be meaningful?

As a matter of fact, ritual has no meaning whatever in spiritual awakening. It was and is used for many reasons, but mostly by those in religious hierarchies who need and use them for discipline and control. As an example, in Soto Zen they teach that in order to be yourself, you should just do something with no goal in mind, as in their famous "just continuously polish the stone," or as in "when you eat, just eat"; and yet they apply all sorts of rituals when they sit down to a meal.

True spiritual practice comes from being totally true to Universal Nature, and it is when you embody its Truth that you see things as they truly are, and it is there that you find your true self. Another Zen saying says, "One should be as the frog." When you understand the concept of sitting with no goal, as the frog who just sits and is a frog, you awaken enlightenment. This is meaningful practice!

I gather then that there is nothing we should take to our pillows. Is that correct?

In Pure Mind practice, as well as a few others, there are many times when thinking about the words of a sage, an enlightened being, or even a teacher can be of great value. At your pillow just think about the words for a moment and let them go. This lets them soak in and will allow the significance of their truth to arise calmly. Never try to hurry your thought process. "Meditation is like watering dry soil; it takes time to seep in and the roots to grow."

Awakening is the natural effect of your cumulative efforts. Therefore it is best never to stop trying. Whether awakenings come quickly or slowly, they will come, but you cannot force them. As with a tree sapling you planted, it will grow in its own time. Your job is to dig the hole, water and fertilize the tree, then protect it as best you can. That much is your part, but the way and time it takes to grow is the tree's affair stemming from its True Nature. It comes down to this: just practice in the right way with the right attitude, conduct, effort, and leave awakening enlightenments to Universal Nature. Do this and you will also be at peace with your practice.

Without a teacher or guide and with no community nearby, how does one start to practice?

Of course there are many ways to begin, but whichever way one chooses, it must be respectful. The word virtue comes to mind as a starting point and foundation for one's practice. Creating a virtuous foundation of caring not to harm any living thing by word, action, or thought shows great respect and puts us immediately in harmony with all life and Universal Nature. When our words and deeds come from kindness, our meditation practice becomes rather simple, because we've placed peace in our minds and we begin to quiet. This allows our hearts to open. This kindness and caring* is a start for it can turn all life experiences into practice.

Taking this discussion one step further, it may be said that the next step might be moderation. Most people live a life of excess, which is a very deep swamp from which a lotus flower must grow to enter sunshine's wisdom. Moderation in eating, speech, and sleep help bring a balance of forces into the inner life.

In starting a meditation practice by oneself, do not look at another student's practice habits, because you cannot see his mind. It is hard enough to watch your own mind while striving towards freedom. So begin meditation practice by concentrating on your breath when you sit and you'll come to realize that you can develop this mindful concentration exercise in everyday life and grow steadily in harmony with wisdom.

*Moral action is admirable; it benefits all parties, but it does not rid the doer of delusion nor is it, of itself, enlightenment.

Always practice with the right attitude, conduct, and **effort and leave the rest to Universal Nature. It is important to understand that the attaining of freedom (liberation in Buddhism) is dependent on one's own efforts, but it is an enlightened guide's words that makes it possible.

** Proper effort is not the effort to make something special happen either on your pillow or in everyday life. It is, instead, the effort to be acutely aware and awake in each and every moment, the effort to make each activity of our lives meditative, and to overcome defilements.

There is an old world saying that "The faltering student is the one whose eyes are fixed upon the heavens because his feet are stuck in the mud." It is the guide who recognizes your mired state and lifts you out of the mud to be once again on your joyful way.

Have you had a student who has failed, and if so, what were the reasons?

Yes! The reasons were many, but possibly the overriding reasons were his inability to see the practice as anything but an ordeal, an inconvenience, and his lack of understanding the necessity to get beyond his own desires. Without the patience to pass through his desires, he remained in the category of a person of sensations and not of the spirit. So he remains today on the suffering level of those who imagine that worldly feelings, especially desire, are sublime.

Part three Questions and Answers

Many times I find that I need a glossary of terms and words to understand what Zen commentators are trying to say. Why don't they speak to us in words we can easily understand?

Simply because most of what they say comes from the Buddhist and/or Zen texts. This is the language they learn to speak. Would you not try to learn the language of a foreign country if you planned to live there? You will remain as an alien with no chance of learning unless you learn the language and the meanings behind the language. After doing so, you will be able to understand and, if you choose, to interpret the texts for yourself. For example, when Thich Nhat Hanh speaks of a rose being garbage, he is asking you to see the garbage (fertilizer) in the rose, and thus to understand that the rose is garbage and garbage, the rose. Here we have a great example of being and becoming, of oneness, and impermanence. We, too, are made up of garbage, both in our bodies and our thoughts. In our practice we learn to convert the energy we get from our garbage (thoughts of hate, desire, greed, etc.) to acts of kindness, love, and compassion.

There seem to be many paths or disciplines that expect a herd mentality from their students. They therefore teach a strict set of rules and rituals to be followed in order to reach enlightenment. Does the Pure Mind Path differ?

There is only one Pure Mind Path, and the heart of it is so very simple. That said, it should be added that with this practice, no two students experience their paths in the same way. Each person's path has its own characteristics according to his individual veils. The teaching path twists and turns in response to the particular events the person must experience to allow him to lift those veils.

Experience shows that the majority of students spend most of their time understanding and evaluating differences between their aggregate self, their self nature, and Universal Nature or their true Self.

Their greatest and possibly hardest task is recognizing and setting aside their illusionary moments which are governed by their senses and interpreted by their egos, and focusing on their moments of awakened clarity reached while striving for eternal life, these moments being governed by Universal Nature.

Zen is a miniaturized adaptation of many religious and spiritual practices. Even though its priests and teachers of today along with their practices would be unrecognizable to its founders, they do say or quote many wise things, often without a real understanding of their meaning. Zen is a processed, chewed up, and regurgitated religion that will fill you up, but does not have any nutritional value.

Therefore, like most processed foods, Zen will not do you any good for the long haul. Some of their teachers emphasize one premise that is wholly correct and that is "just let things go" or "rest with things as they are." Here we have the heart of many a spiritual practice. Give up clinging to all dualistic things and thinking such as love and hate, good and bad, beautiful and ugly, sweet and sour, etc. Most importantly, one cannot live any spiritual path according to the ways of "worldly" people. Desire, indulgence, fear, aversion, anger, dissatisfaction, and the king of all—expectation—are the ruination of any practice. A student must live his practice cutting through these dualistic defilements. Doing so results in a life of tranquility and acute awareness, relieved of both elation and sorrow. "When you feel anger, laziness, or know envy, or feel put upon, ask yourself: What is the use of this? Then let it go!!!"

Pure Mind accepts these premises as important aspects of spiritual practice, including its own Wheel, but it goes far beyond any other practice in its awakened and stated reasons for existence and necessary complexity of practice. On the other hand, it does not share the views of those who insist on rituals or "old time religion" for the sake of conformity.

Emptiness is a concept I find hard to understand.

Could you comment on its value?

For most students, reaching the understanding of emptiness proves to be their first momentous awakening. Sorrow, happiness, pain, love, hate, competitiveness, expectation, desire, and many other states or emotions have no basic nature of their own except what we give to them. Therefore, we call them empty. Recognizing our own minds as their source, we also recognize their impermanence, so when they arise, we can let them pass by and not attach to them, thus avoiding most causes of suffering. "The emptier you become, the fuller you get."

In what form will an In-Perpetuum Being reveal himself to me?

He will appear like any other human, that is, a prisoner in this world of forms, but unlike them his form and consciousness can be set aside. Thankfully, this freedom decisively outweighs his imprisonment. If you study him carefully, he will appear to have two centers of consciousness, one human and one not. He may speak from one in any moment and from the other in the next moment. This accounts for any apparent contradictions one may envision. Whether speaking from one consciousness or the other, however, his words and actions will never conflict with Universal Truth.

The highest form of consciousness is not seeing dark or light, you and me, but instead recognizing that your mind is what defines these differences and all relationships. The relationship between a student and his teacher is also this way.

How do you answer the people who insist that each person must find his own way?

In modern day society it is fashionable to stress freedom to choose a path to one's awakening. This is most unfortunate, because those who speak do not reveal (because they obviously do not know) the true meaning of freedom or how one should go about choosing his path.

Today's other very popular thesis is that "each person will or must find his own correct path." This is simply ridiculous! Through cultural conditioning humans have come to believe that ***"what they like is what they need."*** They take apart a proven discipline and pick what conforms to their mental and/or physical comfort zone and call it their path. If they cannot find anything existing that fits their preconceptions, they feel free to change another's philosophical tenets or invent a practice that does fit. Today, due to humanity's place in its evolution, man needs a reincarnate to arrange and implement circumstances that will lead him to knowledge and awakening experiences.

*~feelings are barriers
to your search,
not conductors of it.~*

What do you feel is the greatest difference in the approach of a Pure Mind student and those of other practices or religions?

Surrender and consumption! In all spiritual, religious, living, and sexual pursuits, a deep and fulfilling climax can only be brought to fruition by surrendering your ego and fears to allow these experiences to consume you. In almost all cases man tries to dictate his needs and desires onto the practice of love, life, learning, religion, or spirituality. He spends most of his new found passion on consuming that which he desires. This way of being, without question, always results in failure. Spirituality, love, life, etc., offers so much more to man than man can offer to them. The absolute and only way to succeed in these pursuits is for you to surrender totally to whatever you are doing and allow it to consume you fully. Recognize your hunger, so that you may satisfy its craving. *The desire to learn for the purpose of quenching your "ghost" is your test!*

All that you have said is very exciting and different but how can I know that it's true?

Don't ask us, ask yourSelf. We have spoken and you have heard or read the Truth. But as you have learned, this is not the way to understand or to know anything. You must seek your answers beyond yourself from yourSelf. When Pure Mind practice has prepared you for understanding, then, in their time, the answers will come, and you will awaken to experience for yourself and know that the Truth is as we have said.

Part Four

Additional Topics and Miscellaneous Ranting

~My teacher's teaching loom.
Sadly, not even love can
repay its weaving.~

dawn's early light!
my moments
reflecting its moments......

Part four   Letter   1

This is a copy of a letter Mahan Agass sent a friend who created some different experiences during his silent sitting meditation. He explained that after glancing through a book on Tibetan Yoga, he performed some of its exercises resulting in strong energy with heat. He asked Mahan's opinion of the exercises and on whether to continue.

Yoga practices of psychic heat or inner fire and Bardo both derive from the Yogic Path of Form. These practices are advanced spiritual paths, different from the advanced path of Zen which is called the Formless path. They are considered by us as being of equal worth, since both aim for experiencing the Void by beings still within the realm of non-void. In olden times (7th century) which of the two approaches would be taken by the student was strictly in the hands of his Lama and depended upon his assessment of the student's character and ability. Though the Formless path may seem to Zen practitioners to be a higher spiritual practice, IT IS BESET WITH A MYRIAD OF DEEP PITFALLS. This is partly because of the absence of a DIVERSITY OF MEANS (being stuck in a single meditation practice surrounded by unenlightened "robes") and the difficulty of conveying in words the steps to be traversed. It is too easy for those whose practice is formless to confuse success with mental wooziness and a vague (though at times profound) happy or blissful feeling that everything is OK and all's right with the world!

Correct practice of the Yoga of psychic heat produces a powerful psychic energy force and is, therefore, one of the primary exercises within the advanced Pure Mind Path. It was formerly also used for its practical side effect, the generation of physical heat to protect those living in caves.

Briefly, in the Yoga of the Bardo, the yogi learns to traverse dying, death, after-death, and rebirth with no break in his stream of consciousness.

These are but two of six Yoga practices on the Path of Form. The one that may awaken you to who I am is the Yoga of Consciousness Transference. This is where a student learns how to transfer his consciousness from body to body and/or place to place, and to enter upon a state of rebirth of his own choice.

Back to the practice of psychic heat and to answer your question. This practice takes years to master and is almost always only successful in solitude. It combines Hatha Yoga with visualizations and breathing exercises. The true and most successful method is by making the prime object of your visualization the syllable *Ah*. By controlled breathing and intense mental concentration you cause a hot blaze that turns into a flame that fills your body, and then with much practice, experience, and guidance you can expand it and fill the universe before it dissipates (here, my friend, is a partial explanation of what you believe to be fantasy, astral travel). Here again, you see why it is a defilement within Pure Mind to play "games" with energy, the one thing that builds our vessel. There were in the old days (maybe today also) contests among newly accomplished "adepts" to see how much heat they could generate by melting snow under their bodies or by drying wet clothing.

Let me just say two important things: 1) In the days when the foundations of Zen were formed, following the Formless (Zen) path involved yoga practices of the mind and included a support system of detailed visualizations and/or manipulation of the psychic centers and channels. This does not exist today because, among other things, Zen does not have accomplished Lamas able to gauge a student accurately and provide appropriate instruction nor do they have the ability of acute observation. You see, without specific visual changes like those created when practicing the Path of Form, there is the great danger that students, like those of Zen along with other diluted practices, will delude themselves by exaggerating their progress, and further, believe they are liberated because they became "aware" without manifesting and embodying their "awakenings."

2) There is no one path that is truer than another, because they all stem from Pure Mind ideals and practice. To be successful in their efforts true practitioners must eventually bring together these incomplete splinters and begin the practice of the Pure Mind Path. Depending on which splinter a student chose to begin with, his path was made longer or shorter, more or less direct. Zen arose from China and Japan, Vajrayana from Tibet, but they only differ in their stink of outward trappings and the huge gap that those trappings created between the true Lamas of yesterday and the watered down imitations of today. So to play around with very powerful forces without the guidance of a genuine master is dangerous both to oneself and many others. Unchecked, these energies have the power to destroy. Learning the practice through books without prior instruction, yoga training and understanding, and a truly competent teacher is not only useless, but a danger to one's health.

Have a nice day!

God

Existence *itself* always was and always will be; there can never be a non-existence of existence. This is in opposition to all other states that exist only in a time frame and until energized they were only latent possibilities that resided *within* existence itself. All forms or thoughts that exist reach a point of non-existence and, therefore, you can say that those things either will exist or have existed. In what category would you put God? If you say he exists he will reach a non-existent state, and is therefore not eternal.

Whether you use your own criteria or accept someone else's definition of God, there are and always were reasons for His coming into being. In most religions, as well as in personal definitions, it is as "the" creator. This is the perfect role for humanity to assign to their conception of God, for now we have the opportunity to laden Him with what should be our responsibilities. He is the "one" responsible for all creation, and therefore, He must take responsibility for all that takes place within it, all the good, all the evil, all the suffering, and all the consequences. Since we place Him in a constant state of awareness and "doing," we can ask Him to alter conditions for our benefit, relief, and comfort. He is the perfect scapegoat for all our actions or inaction, the one "somebody" who is ultimately to blame, and yet we must not be too harsh for He is the one who can change the outcome, and so through our prayers we implore Him to do so. When a player of some "sport"* gets down on his knees and thanks the Lord for his victory, does he really believe that God made a choice between him and his opponent? How did God choose? Was He keeping score on past deeds or prayers? Was the game played on a Sunday, and did He have the day off in order to watch the game? It seems that we place a very large burden of chores and choices on His shoulders.

In many ways we are led to believe, either by our own needs or the wish of others, that He is the creator of all reality, the realities of everyday fortunes, misfortunes, births and deaths, happiness and sorrow. If this is truth, then how can He be reality itself? Did he create Himself? Of course not, for if He was created, then He is not God. He is a thing, a word-thing that man created to give himself answers, answers which otherwise are seemingly beyond his capability of knowing. This word "God" has no connection to any form or reality. It is an illusion resting on the incorrect interpretation of reality. That reality is man's need to fulfill Universal Nature's law of awakening, for when nothing is awakened, nothing can be manifested and, therefore, nothing can be known.

*I refuse to call an action that pits two unevenly matched beings, such as any form of hunting or bullfighting "a sport or sporting event." It's murder, plain and simple.

Part four   God

People who are fond of an easy way to think and live are not capable of a living practice aimed at awakening, and so they choose easy answers, illusions based on belief systems without any base in reality. In other words they choose to believe in a mysterious, unknowable, sometimes benevolent, all-powerful "God."

Did you ever notice that the hierarchy of all religions talk of God speaking through them or directly to them. They are, therefore, only responsible to "Him" and are not accountable for their actions or the consequences. That they can only be held responsible by Him, not by you or by me, is their egos' saving face. No responsibility, therefore no judgment, that is their shelter. It is no wonder that governments, corporations, churches, and other power structures adopt this "somebody other than me" umbrella to operate under.

If you truly need a God in your life, then say that God is the itness of all things. A God cannot be personal, or a thing, for a "God" cannot be the "it." He would have to be the sum, the totality "it"self. Those who call the itness "God" need a divine all-powerful form that they can envision and turn to for universal answers and also help solve problems they themselves cannot. With seemingly no other place to turn, people create(d) God illusions which they hold as separate from themselves.

Totality is indefinable, because definition requires a drawing of boundaries, and the totality has no limits; it is infinite. *We cannot conceive of the infinite, for whatever is conceived by mind is limited, finite.* We cannot picture a boundaryless existence, but it is so, and whether we can see it or not makes no difference.

The logical mind demands definition and clearly defined limits. This is why most of humanity cannot reach what lies beyond the known. Those who choose to "know God" unfortunately become delusional having chosen to accept a man-made definition. Our languages are not meant to express the indefinable, so don't try!

~ah yes, God;
so many
fingerprints~

The Christ
Jesus of Nazareth, later to be known as The Anointed, The Jewish Messiah, was reincarnated as another child of Mary and Joseph (many texts from the East support this contention), this one coming rather late in their lives. Twice spoken of in the Bible until the age of seven, he disappears for about twenty-three years. Reappearing at age thirty, he fulfills John the Baptist's vision and becomes his hand-picked disciple to carry on his work. After

John the Baptist passes the mantle on to Jesus, John chooses to turn inward and lead a life of silence, in effect disappearing from all his followers. On the day of Jesus' initiation in the River Jordan, John the Baptist was heard to say, "...now take over my work and I will disappear. It is enough!" Jesus' ministry lasted for approximately three years until his crucifixion and, fortunately for his ardent followers, perceived resurrection.

Neither the Christian Bible nor Christianity itself has anything to say about his life from the age of seven to age thirty, his awakening, or how and where he was taught. Where did he disappear to after he was seen by as many as eight different people walking the streets a few days after his "resurrection rising to the kingdom of heaven"? We must ask ourselves, how can Christianity be complete with these and so many more unanswered questions? Ironically "the greatest story ever ("never" would be a better choice) told" is one with a beginning and an end, but has no middle, no hows, no why. It just creates further questions, myths, and distorts facts to augment the belief system already in place.

By preaching mainly to the uneducated masses in words whose meanings they could not relate to, Jesus left everything he said up to interpretation by a materialistic people who had no experience with the spiritual dimensions. Therefore, the words he spoke took on a meaning completely different from what he intended. They remain as confused misinterpretations by people whose only perspectives came from dualistic thinking and an exceedingly vengeful God. One of his greatest miscalculations involved the apostles he chose. Having been selected to communicate his teachings, they further misconstrued his already poorly understood words. They were an uneducated, simple people whose burden it was to spread ideas they themselves could not comprehend. In trying to fulfill the Jewish prophecy of a Messiah who would redeem our sins and relieve our suffering, the people and then the church hierarchy have, in fact, created a greater quantity of both.

At a young age, Jesus was recognized as someone special and was taken to the East. While in what was then known as Kashir, he studied for many years in a Buddhist monastery. Taking the vows of a monk, which included a vow of poverty, he settled down for long periods of meditation practice. As he reawakened, his understandings of Hindu-based Buddhism which stressed the Four Noble Truths of suffering, impermanence, compassion, and reincarnation were clarified.

Shortly after reawakening to the truth of his being a reincarnate, and after further awakenings to a

Part four   God   7

mission of becoming a teacher, he unfortunately left the monastery prior to becoming fully reelightened. It is hard to know just how deep his newly awakened reenlightenments were, for not only was this most important part of his life omitted from the Bible, but this very popular text is only a consolidation of diverse writings chosen by the hierarchy of the time to pacify a ruler who insisted on having a final definitive version. These books of the Bible were written a long time after his departure from Jerusalem, the supposed facts were mostly hearsay, and they were recorded by ignorant people.

Following a path through the mountains, Jesus reached the place he was searching for. This was the place where some of the "lost tribes of Israel" lived and prospered. He felt at home and created his first ministry there. As an excellent orator he was gathering a flock, but after awhile he felt an urgency to return to the area where he was born. Continuing his travels to his homeland, he continued to preach, and his trail can still be partially identified today by the towns and villages named after him. It took him a longer time than most who traveled this route due to his popular teaching practice. When he reached Jerusalem, Jesus was thirty years old.

It is one thing for a man to be a great orator, but another thing entirely when the words he speaks are wantonly construed to fulfill the prophecy that people desperately wanted fulfilled. Having never fully awakened, it could be said that his greatest problems were first, trying to teach truths he himself didn't fully understand, and second, because of speaking like an Indian Buddha, there was no communion with the Jews who were rooted in the materialistic world. As an example, when Jesus said, "I am the king of the Jews," he was using a metaphor. He was not speaking of an existing kingdom of this world, but neither his followers, who took his words literally, nor his enemies understood. They interpreted his words in terms of an earthly kingdom, not understanding that what he said referred to another symbolic dimension. Consequently, he was creating a situation in which the Jews believed he aspired to be king, and his enemies believed that a Jew was threatening their monarchy.

Another small example relates to the time that Jesus went to the mountains to meditate in order to deepen his enlightenment. The going and returning forty days later were faithfully recorded, but what did he do? What happened when he began his preaching again? How were the practices of meditation and enlightenment understood? Furthermore, we have Jesus' intolerance for the rich which possibly came about from his vows of poverty and simplicity as a Buddhist monk, again suggesting, along with many other wrongly understood precepts, the shallowness of his enlightenments.

So many unanswered questions. So many things unknown, the whole story shabbily penned, and as the facts are incomplete the religion itself is incomplete and is thereby in a constant struggle with opposites and partial truths. If viewed from Hindu-based Buddhism or Pure Mind awakened experiences, things such as the trilogy of the Father, Son, and Holy Ghost, heaven, hell, the devil, and many other "mysteries" along with the so-called miracles of the Christian/Judaic religions are quite easily explained and understood.

Finally, in an attempt to communicate with greater clarity Jesus generally abandoned his philosophical approach and preached along more social and political lines. But the damage was beyond repair. It was too late, because the Jews of yesterday, as they are today, are only concerned with this world. For them nothing transcends this world, it only continues. They understand a totally different language which doesn't have room for the spiritual dimensions. Probably the person who understood Jesus most clearly was the Roman governor, Pilate, but due to his position, he chose to wash his hands of the whole affair and disappear from the scene leaving his priests in charge.

In any case, for the sake of both sides Jesus had to die. For the Romans, it was simply a matter of necessity and good politics, preventing, they believed, a possible future uprising. For the Jews, either Jesus died and the miracle of resurrection took place, or the whole newly founded religion died. The prophecy called for the coming of Christ, his crucifixion, and further resurrection. If this was not done, then the Jews neither would nor could have believed in Jesus either as the Christ or as a prophet. They never wanted to see the man who was always attempting meditation because he was struggling to deepen his enlightenment, nor did they recognize a teacher who was preaching to those who were non-spiritual, not at all philosophical, illiterate, and totally literal.

Being seen as somewhat of a troublemaker, Jesus had to be made silent. There is much written in the East explaining what seemed to be the "death" of Jesus on the cross. For a practitioner of yoga, what was done was quite common and holds no mystery. The fact that he was speared by a Roman guard and blood flowed while on the cross proved he was alive, for blood does not flow from a dead body. For those interested in the techniques that helped Jesus appear dead to the followers, it is suggested that you read and study the Yogis of India, those who carry on age-old traditions which can include the practice of slowing down the body's functions so it appears that there is a stoppage of the heart, breathing, and pulse. It was the very same exercise and practice that Jesus had mastered earlier in his studies in the East.

When the crucifiers of Jesus believed him dead, they took him down and gave his remains to his followers. They, in turn, rubbed an ointment on him and wrapped his body in a thin muslin cloth. Two followers then placed his wrapped body in a cave and blocked the entrance with a boulder. Needing the followers of Jesus to believe he was healed and resurrected, the Essenes helped Jesus recover from his wounds during the three days he remained in the cave. When he was healed, he disappeared. It was this disappearance that led to the belief in his resurrection and ascent to heaven. But, having shown himself to his disciples, he had to disappear from the country, otherwise he would have been crucified once more, so he left for the last time and traveled to India.

Jesus eventually resettled in Kashmir where he lived in human form until he was one hundred and two years old. The whole Arabic world called him Esua. In Kashmir he is know as Yousa-Asaf. His tomb, which can still be seen today, bears his name, footprint, and a plaque proclaiming his arrival in Kashmir. In today's calendar it loosely translates to the year three C.E.

Jesus tried to communicate with people of the West; this, along with his crucifixion, is the true essence of the story. He believed the crucifixion was necessary, because it was the only way his apostles could carry on the teaching while continuing to worship who they believed he was, and it was also necessary for what he and his followers were attempting to convey.

This whole fiasco changed the way Jesus lived forever. From then on, he lived in Kashmir continually for approximately seventy years. He did not travel, and he didn't preach. He was not seen as a prophet, priest, or minister. Instead he lived with a small group of awakened beings, worked, and studied silently. He was turning inward to the spiritual dimensions, in search of much deeper enlightenment and the strengthening of his energy vessel that had lost much during the years in Judea. This esoteric tradition lives today and remains well hidden.

The Dead Sea Scrolls, originally written and preserved by the Essenes, as well as the Koran, are more accurate than the Old and New Testaments of today. They tell a much different version than the writers of the Bible. The Christian hierarchy cannot and will not compromise its tenets, because Christianity is exoteric, only concerned with the outer material world. It is always the way of exoteric thinkers to wear down and then destroy everything that is esoteric and, therefore, a disturbing threat to materialism. If Jesus would reincarnate today as the Messiah, he would, by necessity, be crucified again, but this time by the Christian church. Christianity is totally exoteric; it is the Establishment, and its leaders are more like the priests of old Rome trying to protect their interests.

It would be correct to believe in Jesus, if you leave out Christianity. You would enrich your understanding if and when you viewed him as he truly was, a reincarnated In-Perpetuum Being who, until the age of fifty-something, was only somewhat reawakened.

~The Prophecy

A simple man awakened to life,
as it might be,
and from this awakening
a ministry grew.
A prophecy had long ago
come from their "God"
so all the people gathered to hear,
if it was indeed "coming true."

This preacher having studied the
mysteries of love, kindness, and woe,
sought with his preaching to give

people understanding, a more
important reality and an inner glow.
His followers who thought him true,
heard his heart but not its soul,
the words were plain, but they hadn't a clue.
This preacher spoke words so foreign,
yet so tender, their hearts wiped clear,
and so all the hills filled with those who
needed to hear about a path sliced open
for them to sit with a God whose
existence they held so dear.

This "prophet's" voice was silenced
because his words were from an
infinite dimension, yet the
people rallied, crying, " How could his
words be false or his thinking askew?
Did he not show us our God's
prophecy was true?"~

Glossary of Words and Phrases

Absolute Truth —Truth that cannot change. One that is not open for interpretation by man.

Adept/mystic — One who has attained the highest level of spiritual enlightenment. Highly skilled.

Altered states of consciousness — Detached states of awareness stemming from other than the human mind.

Asceti(c)(ism) — A person who leads a life of contemplation and rigorous self-denial usually for religious purposes; his disciplines.

Compassion — A true understanding of cause and effect in relation to a persons actions.

Consciousness — The totality of human self reflexive awareness. Mind stuff. The condition or power of perception, awareness, apprehension. There are different levels of consciousness, from the simple sense perception of inanimate matter, to the consciousness of basic life forms, to the consciousness of human expression, to the spiritual states of intuitive knowledge leading to Universal consciousness of the oneness of all things.

Concentration — Its essence is nondistractedness, its goal is to focus the thought flow by fixing the mind on a single object or meditation topic.

Ecstasy — A feeling of overpowering rapture or joy, believed to arise by stopping the energy waves of sensory and rational knowing, fantasy, dreams and memory.

Ecstasy, mystical — Ecstasies which allow a transcendence of the usual self-identity. A second more valuable re-identification takes places initiating one into or deepening one's spiritual participation.
Ecstasy, esoteric — A feeling of rapture coming from awakening experiences outside ourselves. Or the joy felt when being in a spiritual state outside ourselves.
Ecstasy, exoteric — Sensory dominated self-conscious feeling of rapture or joy achieved with drugs, sensual sensations, perfume, crystal clear night skies etc.
Ego — The external personality or sense of "I" and "mine." Individual identity and all the things that give one that sense of I-ness.
Embody — To give bodily form to. To incorporate into ones being.
Enlightenment — The result of awakening. The ultimate awakened knowledge. The experience-nonexperience resulting in the realization of the oneness of Self and Universal Nature which exists beyond time, form and space.
Esoteric — From inner/internal or higher hidden places.
Essence — The ultimate, real and unchanging nature of a thing or being.
Eternal Being — One who has created the karmic effect of perpetual life cycles. An energizer of latent possibilities. A creator.
Exoteric — From the physical/external through

the senses.

External meditation — 1) To communicate with other forms becoming the recipient of their knowledge. 2) The harnessing of some previously uncontrolled forces. 3) In praise of, or devotional prayer. Using ritual prayer as a means of communication. 4) Reaching out.

Guru — A teacher or guide.

Immanent — Indwelling; present and operating within.

Inperpetuum Being — An eternal being reincarnated in a physical form.

Insight — Seeing things as they are.

Internal meditation — 1) To awaken by becoming the recipient of knowledge. 2) To reach spiritual dimensions, through meditation, allowing the awakening of Absolute Truth. For example, the unity of all phenomenal diversity and the presence of a Universal Nature that resides beyond yet permeates all other natures. 3) Flowing in.

Karma — 1) Law of cause and effect. 2) A reason for responsibility.

Kundalini (yoga) — The primordial energy in everyone which lies at the base of the spine and through the practice of yoga, rises up through the chakras and awakens every one of them.

Manifest — To show or reveal. Having form. Opposite of transcendent.

Mandala — A diagram or model having a common center for the purpose of meditation. Using images and colors in the same way as mantras use sound

Mantra — 1) Translates to "a tool for thinking," a "thing which creates a mental picture." With its sound it calls forth its content into a state of immediate reality. Like the true poet whose words create actuality, mantras call forth and unveil somehing real. Their words do not talk — "they act!" 2) In Tantra, a word-symbol which is a sacred sound. The inner vibrations set up by this sacred sound, along with its association in the consciousness of the practitioner, open the mind to the experience of higher dimensions.

Meditation — 1) a path needed for the person who seeks to go beyond the limiting goals of the everyday world. 2) not an end in itself but a means to whatever end one has chosen. 3) In its most widely accepted definition is a withdrawal into an inner dimension from which one undertakes no outward action but loses oneself in another state of being totally divorced from the concerns of daily life and this world. 4) the technique which deliberately produces forms of ecstasy, experiential states of consciousness, which can be used to learn about self and this world and to develop one's mental potential and extend its possibilities. 5) Yogic — it is the temporary stoppage of the waves of the mind. Buddhist-arresting or calming of the minds contents resulting in ecstasy.

Meditative object — 1) The goal of meditation

glossary 5

skills. 2) Physical, mental, auditory, visual etc. focusing devices which serve in meditation.

Meditative state — 1) Transcendence of humanness or our normal worldly mind to be conscious in and/or through one of the many spiritual dimensions. 2) Gives us power by allowing access to a deeper more all-knowing aspect of the psyche which advises us in its own interest. 3) It is not the meditation technique. One cannot learn it. It is growth, a flowering that must come through you with basic transformation. You grow towards the meditative state.

Mindfulness — Is the state of being in this very moment, at this very moment. In this state we are able to achieve clear awareness.

Mudra — Esoteric hand gestures which express specific energies or power.

Mystic(al)(ism) — A particular form of direct knowledge. Mystics maintain that one must transcend one's ordinary, limited identity, by surrendering attachment to one's usual selfhood as the primary requirement for experiencing "oneness" and ecstatic joy.

Practitioner — A student of meditation.

Reality — What a culture, group, individual, considers to exist.

Reality, spiritual — the immaterial, transcendent, mysterious aspect of existence.

Shaman — Believers in the universal web of power that supports all life. That all elements of the environment are alive and all have their source of power in the spirit world. That they can access vital survival information and knowledge through what they call "spirit journeys." An intermediary between man and divine forces.

Shamanism — Journeying within imagination to contact the spirit world or the world of the spirit self: contacting the universal source of all knowledge by going deeply within oneself. Questions or matters of great concern are answered through ecstatic journeys allowing a broader vision by bypassing the primal sensory and materialistic world.

Science — Our dominant system of cultural knowledge. It seeks to know in its own way and, therefore, produces a reality based solely on its perimeters resulting in its own appropriate reality experience that addresses the "about" and "of" things but never the essence of those things.

Spirit guide — All species and forms have a combined mutual spirit. Black bears have one spirit self, as all other families of bears have. This goes for all species, animate as well as inanimate. To learn about the habits of the buffalo, for example, one must befriend the buffalo spirit self.

Spiritual dimensions — where can be found the reality that exists within all phenomena yet transcends it. The mysterious other side of ordinary secular reality.

Tantr(a)(ic) — A ritualistic system of meditation. This tradition is strongly oriented toward human

glossary

experiential potential and describes spiritual development in terms of practitioner, meditation path, and result. The meditation path purifies the practitioner; as a result the practitioner reaches a state that arises as an effect of a particular Tantric practice.

Tools — Any and all meditation techniques.

Transcend(ence) — Going beyond. A shift from ordinary into altered, discrete states of consciousness and possibly moving to a non-material spiritual level of existence.

Transformation — induced change or reversal in the ordinary mode of thinking or action.

Unconditional love — A love that is given freely with no expectations of any kind.

Vehicle — The formula, religion, belief system, science, etc. that utilizes meditation to reach beyond the normal human condition or consciousness.

Yoga — 1) the oldest definition; an achieved skill in which one trains oneself, by harnessing some force in order to utilize that power to enhance the success of some undertaking or adventure. 2) seeking to transcend duality by or in union with Self. 3) Tibetan—seeking inner unification through meditation.

Yogi/yogin — practitioner of a form of yoga.

Afterword

Having read this book you should be aware that it means nothing unto itself. As we have said and/or quoted many times throughout, words are useless in matters of spiritual awakening. True learning comes from doing. We have only provided a beginning outline for physical practice and the philosophical seeds to begin your quest. You must learn for yourself the Truth of your life purpose by living the Pure Mind Path with a dedication of faithful practice. Strength of resolve helps invoke spiritual enlightenment and provides the deep inner faith needed to attain the state of perpetual existence. While you're in a meditative state the Breath of Universal Life provides you with the understanding of why, who, and what you are through awakening experiences. This may seemingly take a very long time, but seriously, what better can you do with the time remaining in your life?

The first step and all steps that follow are up to you. We can help guide you with answers, suggestions and updates as they occur through the resources listed on the back of this page. We hope that you will take the necessary steps inward and in turn be successful in finding your teacher and forever put to rest your "hungry ghost" that Universal Nature has so thoughtfully provided.

Subscription Information:
Wheelbarrow, the Pure Mind Foundation's newsletter, along with any book revisions, updates, or additions may be obtained from the Pure Mind Foundation's web site:
http://www.puremind.com
email: puremind_az@yahoo.com

To order this book in a loose-leaf laser print format use the Pure Mind web site as shown above.

Questions regarding the contents of this book, the Pure Mind Foundation, its polices, and/or mission will be answered at the Pure Mind Foundation's web site, see above, or by writing to:

Pure Mind Foundation
1228 Westloop
#320
Manhattan, KS 66502
or, email us at:
puremind@networksplus.net

Proof of Purchase

Name _____

Address _____

City_____ State_____ Zip_____

E-mail Address _____

Phone # _____

Send in this proof of purchase to access the Pure Mind information site. A private combination will be sent to you by either U.S. Mail or E-mail. Thank you for purchasing this book.
